I0137137

WHAT
Season
ARE YOU IN?

© Copyright 2022- Raygan Boster and Joe Pileggi

All rights reserved. Permission is granted to copy or reprint portions for any noncommercial use, except they may not be posted online without permission.

Wyatt House books may be ordered through booksellers or by contacting:

WYATT HOUSE PUBLISHING
399 Lakeview Dr. W.
Mobile, Alabama 36695
www.wyattpublishing.com
editor@wyattpublishing.com

Because of the dynamic nature of the Internet, any web address or links contained in this book may have changed since publication and may no longer be valid.

Cover design by: Josiah Tower and Mark Wyatt

Interior design by: Mark Wyatt

ISBN 13:978-1-954798-08-3

Printed in the United States of America

WHAT
Season
ARE YOU IN?

HOW TO PROSPER IN THE CHANGING SEASONS
THAT GOD BRINGS YOU THROUGH

by
Raygan Boster
&
Joe Pileggi

illustrated by

Josiah Tower

WHP
Word Haven Publishing

Mobile, Alabama

Other books by Joe Pileggi

FEARLESS

Children's Books

NO GREATER LOVE

A SPECIAL NIGHT

THE THIRD DAY

Dedication

I am dedicating this book to three ladies in my life.

The first, of course, is my bride of 51 years, Lori. She is the woman of God that He called alongside me who has been my faithful companion and encourager all these years. Although our marriage has "...walked through the valley of the shadow of death..." more than once, the Lord has been faithful to "...set a table (for us) in the presence of (our) enemies..." and today, "...our cup runneth over"! (taken from Psalm 23)

The second lady in my life is my daughter, Lisa. From a "fuzzy-headed" teenager to the powerful woman of God she is today, Lisa, too, has walked through her valleys. But rather than allowing those valleys to derail her faith, she determined to make what the enemy meant for evil turn for her good. Today, she stands stronger in her faith than ever, ministering God's grace and hope to those who are walking through their valley. She stands as an example to us all, me included, of a faith that perseveres through the storm and produces a Kingdom warrior who will not be denied God's destiny for her life. She epitomizes Bethel's song, "I Raise a Hallelujah": "I'm gonna sing in the middle of the storm, louder and louder, you're gonna hear my praises roar. Up from the ashes, hope will arise. Death is defeated, the King is alive!"

Last, but not least, is Raygan, my granddaughter and co-author of this book. From holding her in my arms as a new-born, to proudly watching her walk across the stage as a high school graduate, I have seen Raygan grow and mature into a dynamic woman of God who has identified her God-given destiny and is pursuing it with reckless abandon. "Resilience" is her theme as you will see in the chapters ahead.

All of these women have lived and walked through the seasons described in this book – multiple times. Their triumph is a message of hope to all who read it, and a warning to the kingdom of darkness: "You gave it your best shot and lost.

"Now it's MY turn!"

Acknowledgments

Writing a book is never a "one-man (or woman) show". Like most things in life, it takes a team. That statement could not be truer in regards to this project.

First, my wife, Lori, must take center stage. Without her encouragement, this work would never have moved from a dream to reality. She has also done hands-on work, helping to type and edit the transcript, not to mention contributing a chapter of her own!

Next, of course, is my beautiful granddaughter, Raygan Boster, who is co-author with me. As a current sophomore at University of Mobile, Raygan's dream (among others) is to be a published author. Well, dream no longer, my dear! Here you are! You will see a perspective of our seasons in life from a teen-ager who has matured far beyond her years! Her chapters bring an enlightenment and hope to our "seasons" of life that only a Godly youth perspective can bring. Excuse me for bragging, but I **am** her Papa!

I met Josiah through a class in which he enrolled and which I taught at our fellowship school. From that has developed a mentoring relationship that has grown into a close friendship.

Josiah has done the artwork you see on the cover as well as the beginning of each "season" section.. As you can see, the colors are stunning and the detail professional. He, too, has added a chapter taken from his own experience of walking through his seasons of life.

I would be remiss if I didn't recognize my publisher, Mark Wyatt, for bringing this project to you. I am honored to call Mark a friend as well as a brother in Christ. He has formed this publishing company as a ministry to new and "struggling" authors who do not have the resources to publish with the larger publishing houses. Thank you, Mark, for your committed, tireless work and your help, counsel, and wisdom in helping me complete this work.

Finally, I want to thank my home church fellowship, GCPHC (Gulf Coast Prayer & Healing Center) for their unwavering support and "cheerleading" from the sidelines when obstacles and discouragement tempted me to "put it on the shelf". You are my family and a part of the "harvest season" described here.

Contents

Summer

Autumn

Introduction

I don't know about you, but the most frequent question I ask God is "Why?" I want to know why He has allowed a certain circumstance or "station" in my life. Or, why He **hasn't** allowed a dream to be realized or promise to be fulfilled. Just like my kids, when they were small, used to ask that same most popular question: "But why?", especially when it involved pain – like their first visit to the dentist (I still ask why on that one!).

If you are one of Father's children asking "why?" from your "dentist's chair", I pray reading this work will shed some light of revelation for you. It all lies in what God calls "seasons". One of the definitions of the word is "a set time". God's explanation is best expressed in Ecclesiates 3:1 in the NAS (New American Standard): "There is *an appointed time* (emphasis mine) for everything. And there is a time for every event under heaven". Then vv.2-8 go on to give examples, i,e, "a time to give birth, and a time to die, a time to plant, and a time to uproot what is planted", etc.

Seasons were not meant to last forever. They are a part of a journey called life. If we will partner with the Lord as He walks us through our seasons, we will grow and mature, as He teaches us His ways and wisdom in each cycle of seasons. If we will agree with David, who said, "My times are in Thy hands..." (Psa. 31:15a, NAS), we can rest in the fact that we couldn't be in better "hands". One of the meanings of "times" there in Strong's Concordance is "(due) season" (Heb. #6256).

By the way, just as in nature, we live through many cycles of the 4 seasons in our lifetime, so, God, in His wisdom, leads us through multiple spiritual "cycles of seasons'. Why? There's that question again. In my opinion, we couldn't handle learning **everything** He wants to teach us in one cycle. Maturity comes gradually, "line upon line, precept upon precept, here a little, there a little" (Isaiah 28:10).

Can you imagine a child learning everything he/she needs to know for maturity in the first year after birth? Wow! They could say to God, "Ok, God. You can take me back to heaven. I've learned everything I need to know. I got it." I am now in my 73rd cycle of the 4 natural seasons. I don't know (and don't care to know) how many spiritual seasons Father has brought me through, but I do know I am still learning and maturing as He and I walk those seasons together.

The second question after "Why?" is "How long?" That will be covered in detail in one of the chapters, but here I only want to emphasize the basic answer: It's up to us. We determine how long we stay in each season. While the natural seasons each last around 90 days, our spiritual season will last as long as it takes for us to learn and mature through what Father is taking us. The quicker we learn (and submit to) His ways, the quicker we will be ready to move into the next season He has for us.

The ultimate season toward which Father wants to take us is our harvest season. That is the season where we reap the benefits of all we've learned from Him through the other 3 seasons. Winter, Spring, and Summer are merely preparation seasons for the fulfillment and manifestation of all Father has promised and the destiny for which He has been preparing us!

Are you ready? It's a journey, sometimes difficult, but worth the effort. This verse seems to speak to this season cycle we walk in: "He who goes to and fro (the journey?) weeping (Winter?), carrying his bag of seed (Spring?), shall indeed come again with a shout of joy (Summer?), bringing his sheaves (harvest?) with him" (Psa. 126:6, NAS).

There is no need to fear this journey, because we will not walk it alone:

"...lo, I am with you always, even to the end of the age." (Matt. 28:20, NAS).

"Be strong and courageous, do not be afraid or tremble at them, for the Lord your God is the One who goes with you. He will not fail you or forsake you...And the Lord is the One who goes ahead of you; He will be with you. He will not fail you or forsake you. Do not fear, or be dismayed." (Deut. 31:6,8, NAS).

"No man will be able to stand before you all the days of your life. Just as I was with Moses, I will be with you; I will not fail you or forsake you." (Joshua 1:5, NAS).

"...for He Himself has said, 'I will never desert you, nor will I ever forsake you.'" (Heb. 13:5b, NAS).

Hey, did you hear that? "**He Himself said**...". I didn't say it. **He** did! Can you depend on what He said? Yeah, I think so: "God is not a man, that He should lie; neither the son of man, that He should repent: hath He said, and shall He not do it? Or hath He spoken, and shall He not make it good?" (Numbers 23:19, KJV).

Ok. Grab His hand and let's start our journey with Him!

Winter

1

WINTER: A TEEN'S PERSPECTIVE

by Raygan Boster

IT'S COLD OUTSIDE

When the temperature drops in winter, it can be kind of a shock sometimes. Where I am from, one day it is seventy degrees outside, then the next it is in the thirties or forties. It can be really hard to adjust to.

The same goes for our spiritual lives. One day you can be feeling the fire for God, then the next it feels like it is completely gone. It is not easy to get used to. When you are in the coldest part of the season, you often sit wishing for the heat to come back, wondering what the purpose of the cold is. However, take heart. It is all for a purpose. That does not mean it will be pleasant, of course. Freezing cold temperatures rarely are. But once the shock fades, you will be able to see more clearly.

Don't just wait for the season to change; work and prepare for when it does. If you don't, you will just end up being in shock once again.

EVERYTHING'S DEAD

We all know that in the midst of winter, all the leaves have fallen, and everything looks dark, dreary, and just dead. Most people see that as almost depressing at times. However, there can be such beauty in it if you know what is happening underneath. What we don't see is the growth that is happening in everything around us. When plants shed their leaves, they are getting rid of the damaged leaves and preparing for the new, healthy leaves to grow in the spring.

The same thing happens in our spiritual lives. When we feel like our relationships and situations are going cold and dead, God is removing the things in our life that are not benefiting us anymore. John 15:2 explains this very well. It says the following: "Every branch in Me that does not bear fruit, He takes away; every branch that does bear fruit He prunes, that it may bear more fruit." The pruning is uncomfortable but incredibly necessary. The hardest part is letting go of what God is removing.

The growth cannot continue unless you release the dead relationships and circumstances in your life. What will come along to replace it after this season will be even better for you, but you have to let the old things pass away in order to receive the new things that God has in store for you.

For me, I have definitely been guilty of holding onto dead things that were needing to be pruned in my life. Honestly, I ended up being more hurt and sad trying to water those dead plants than I would have been if I had just let go at first. On top of that, I missed out on amazing opportunities that could have been really good for me, but I was too focused on saving something that was too far gone.

In the winter, plants get their nourishment mostly from food they stored until spring, when food supply is more accessible. If the plant does not have enough food stored for the entire season, it will eventually die. The same goes for our spiritual self. If we are only putting in enough spiritual food to scrape by, when winter comes around and the food supply dwindles, our spiritual self will wither away.

WILL THIS EVER CHANGE?

When going through a dark season, it is so easy to feel like it will never end or that there is no light at the end of the tunnel. Sometimes this feeling could last for years with no enormous change or relief. However, it all is temporary. Someone once told me, "Everything is temporary. Every emotion is constantly changing. Happiness, sadness, anxiousness, it is all temporary." That honestly changed my entire perspective. The only emotion that will be permanent is when we reunite with Christ and receive His everlasting love, peace, and joy. Don't get too comfortable in this season though. The season will change, and when it does, you need to be prepared for what is coming.

DRESSING FOR THE SEASON

When going out in winter, everyone says to layer up to protect against the cold. This is very true, especially for someone who is cold-natured like me. Honestly, I put on as many layers as possible in order to stay somewhat warm.

We also need to do this spiritually. In the winter season of our spiritual lives, we are much more vulnerable to our surroundings. That being said, in order to protect our spirit from the world and attacks of the enemy, we need to put on many spiritual layers. These layers could be many things, like the armor of God, worship, the Word, Christian fellowship and accountability, and prayer. Of course, these are always important to our spirit, but can help incredibly when you feel disconnected or feel like your situation is overall dead.

2

IT'S COLD OUTSIDE

By Joe Pileggi

As I begin writing this chapter, it is January, 2022. My wife and I live on the Gulf Coast near Mobile, Alabama, but we both grew up in the Northeast part of the U.S.A.: cold country! Lori grew up in Philadelphia, Pa. and I was born and brought up on a dairy farm in upstate NY, in the Mohawk Valley. Winters there are long and frigid. Autumn is spent dreading what is coming! Winter is spent longing, hoping and waiting for the first sign of Spring – a blade of green grass poking through the snow cover, a shoot of a tulip bulb emerging from the frozen "tundra" of Winter.

Winter has really taken a bad rap! No one likes braving the icy North winds and wind chills of January. Even here in "L.A." (lower Alabama) we have extremes. As I awakened on New Year's Day this year, the temperature rose to an unbelievable 79 degrees, a new record! Three days later, (Jan. 4), I took my dog Abby out for her morning walk with the temperature hovering at 27 degrees and a heavy coating of frost everywhere!

Seasons. None are perfect. They each have their extremes. And what is our natural response to those extremes? I don't know about you, but mine is usually to complain. In fact, I've come up with a little jingle that describes my response to those seasonal extremes:

"We complain that Winter is cold.

We complain that Summer is hot.

We complain that Spring is wet.

We complain that Autumn is not!"

I have found that life can follow "seasonal cycles" as well, especially in the spiritual realm. And, as Winter is the harshest season to endure, mainly because of the cold, so I have experienced "winter seasons" in my walk with the Lord that have been equally hard to endure.

Having been in pastoral ministry for more than 50 years, I have known, spoken to, and even counseled many believers (including pastors) as they, too, were walking through their "winter" season.

Sadly, not all persevered through their winter season, becoming a casualty of the hopelessness of ever experiencing the warmth of God's presence and breakthrough from their winter ordeal.

A scientific fact of Winter is that "Winter cold kills more than twice as many Americans as summer heat does." That could probably also be said of those in the body of Christ who abandon their walk with the Lord in a season of spiritual coldness.

What do I mean by the cold of a spiritual winter? For me, this season was a time of the absence of God's presence, feeling like He is a "million miles away." There is no direction for life, no word from the Lord. It is a time of trudging through day after lonely day only because I knew I had to.

How does that happen? Didn't the Lord say "I will never leave you or forsake you" (Heb. 13:5)? The word "forsake" in the New Testament literally means "to leave behind in some place, to desert, abandon" (Strong's Concordance, Gr. #1459). Have you ever felt like you left His presence behind, somewhere, but you didn't know where? It's cold out there (in life) without the warmth of His presence to "warm" us, guide us, and lead us. Why have we been "left out in the cold" and how do we get back into the warmth of His presence?

I believe there are several ways of entry into this spiritually cold season. One is from our own doing: unconfessed sin. Another is brought on through an event or circumstance, possibly not of our own doing. And finally, God Himself could initiate a winter season for His own purposes in our life.

Let's look at the most difficult one first: the winter season we bring upon ourselves through sin. My mind immediately goes to a Biblical example: David.

David was called "a man after God's own heart" (I Sam. 13:14; Acts 13:22). Yet David was overcome with temptation and sinned with Bathsheba resulting in terrible consequences, one of which was the loss of God's presence in his life. In his repentance, David cried out, "Do not cast me away from (Your) presence, and do not take (Your) Holy Spirit from me" (Psa.51:11, NAS). Winter season entered by David's own doing! We know he confessed, was forgiven, and was restored to fellowship with God, but we'll discuss recovery in our next season – Spring!

Another example of this self-inflicted winter season is my own experience.

The darkest of my "winter" seasons began in 1983 and lasted the better part of 20 years. Because of moral sin in my personal life, I was forced to leave the ministry that I loved and was told that, because of it, I would never minister again. That statement, made by my overseer, was the "deep freeze" slap of "winter wind" that threw me into spiritual and emotional turmoil. It was indeed an "arctic blast" that froze me out of seeing any future fulfillment of God's call on my life. In my mind, the purpose for my existence seemed to be over. Despair and hopelessness set in – the "death" of my winter season was in full swing.

Then, in 1984, a powerful prophet came to town. He spoke the most powerful prophetic word over me that I have ever received even to this day. He prophesied, among many other things, that God would call me "out of hiding, as it were (my winter season?), into an Elijah-type ministry." Wow! What a word! Maybe this was my transition into my "spring" season. But then, nothing happened. It was just a temporary "thaw" in my winter. Everything froze back up.

An event, like the storms of life, can be another means of entering a "winter" season with God. A bad business decision, a divorce, a tragic loss of a family member, are just a few examples of entering a winter season that may not necessarily be of your own doing, but is no less "cold" as you walk through it. Where is His presence? This one is more on the emotional level than the spiritual. If we are faithful to His Word, we can be reassured that His presence is there, even if we don't "feel" Him.

I Samuel 3:1(NAS) says, "Now the boy Samuel was ministering to the Lord before Eli. And word from the Lord was rare in those days, visions were infrequent." Here, Samuel was "ministering to the Lord", but hearing a word from the Lord "was rare". Sometimes, we are faithfully serving the Lord and seeking a word from Him for guidance for some other specific event or need. And it seems there is no response. It's "cold outside". We don't sense His presence, but it is not because of any sin. We know that because we've asked and there is no conviction of Holy Spirit. So why is He not speaking?

In those times of silence, when I can't sense His presence or "hear" Him, I have learned that it is a time to trust. Trust what? I have found that my winter season is a season of walking by faith, not by feeling. If something was wrong, Holy Spirit would definitely let me know. It is in these times that I have found great comfort in these words from Proverbs 3:5-6: "Trust in the Lord with all your heart, and do not lean on your own understanding. In all your ways acknowledge Him, and He will make your paths straight (NAS)." The word "trust" there means literally "to be confident or put confidence in" (Strong's Concordance, Heb. #982) the Lord. Be confident that He is there beside you even though you don't feel Him guiding and directing you. You are His precious child and He is a good Father. A good father doesn't let his child veer off the path and fall into a ditch. He assures us in Psalm 32:8, "I will instruct you and teach you in the way which you should go; I will counsel you with My eye upon you"(NAS).

I sense there may be some of you who are reading this that are facing important decisions in your life. You want to make the right decision; you think you know what you should do but you don't sense anything from God one way or the other. Just silence. Check your heart. Ask Holy Spirit if there's anything in your heart that may be blocking or interfering with His voice and presence from reaching you, like unforgiveness, etc. If all is clear, follow Proverbs 3:5 & 6. He WILL direct your path!

In Song of Solomon, chapter 5, verse 6, the bride (representing us, the church) is calling for the Bridegroom

(Jesus) but He's gone: "I opened to my beloved, but my beloved had turned away and gone! My heart went out to him as he spoke. I searched for him, but I did not find him; I called him, but he did not answer me" (NAS). Chapter 3, verses 1 & 2 show a desperation: "On my bed night after night I sought him whom my soul loves; I sought him but did not find him. I must arise now and go about the city; in the streets and in the squares I must seek him whom my soul loves. I sought him but did not find him" (NAS). That's the winter season!

In his book, *Turn Your Season Around*, Darryl Strawberry, former major league baseball superstar, says, "God is working in the middle of your situation even when you don't see any evidence of it. When the desired results you're praying for aren't yet in view, keep praying, trusting, and hoping that God will make a way where there seems to be no way. He is the Way Maker!" (p.74).

The final way we enter our winter season (and we **all** have them) is through God's appointed times. He says in Psalm 75:2, "When I select an appointed time, It is I who judge with equity"(NAS). David was anointed king and then spent the next several years running from Saul and living in caves. The only ones who were loyal to him were a bunch of criminal misfits. Sounds like my plight when I was pastoring, but I digress. He could not understand why he had to run for his life after God had called him and anointed him to lead the nation of Israel. Finally, he had to go beyond his intellectual understanding, relying on the knowledge that God's hand was on his life and say, "My times are in (Your) hand" (Psa. 31:15a, NAS). God will sometimes withdraw the presence of His Spirit and allow us to go through a season of testing to strengthen our trust that He is guiding and directing our life.

It happened to Jesus twice. The first time was when He was driven (by the Spirit) into the wilderness to be tempted by the devil for 40 days. He did not face the devil and his temptations as God; He faced him as a Man. It would have done us no good if He overcame the devil as God. He had already done that when "there was war in Heaven" (Rev. 12:7-9) and He threw the devil out of Heaven down to earth. He had to face him as a Man the same way Adam did and overcome him the way Adam should have – as a man. The writer of Hebrews puts it this way: "For we do not have a high priest who cannot sympathize with our weaknesses, but One who has been tempted in all things as we are, yet without sin" (4:15, NAS). That had to happen so that He could offer Himself as the sinless, spotless Lamb of God. He had to take on the weight of all the sin from Adam to the end of time so that those who come to Him and repent of their personal sin could have it removed "as far as the East is from the West" (Psa. 103:12).

The second time the Father's presence was withdrawn from Him was when He was on the cross and in agony cried out, "My God, my God. Why have You forsaken Me?" (Mt. 27:46). At the moment Jesus took on Himself the load of planet earth's sin and guilt, in my opinion, the Father turned His face away from His Son for the first (and last) time in eternity because He could not look upon the sin that His Son had become. Fellowship between Father and Son, for the first and only time in eternity, was broken. Jesus' agony was not for the physical pain He was suffering but from the Presence of His Father "forsaking" Him. Remember, the word "forsaken" there literally means "to leave behind; desert". It was something Jesus had never experienced and it crushed Him.

Nothing could feel "colder" to our soul than to "lose" (can't feel) the presence of our awesome, loving Father. When God promised Moses, "'My Presence shall go with you, and I will give you rest.'", Moses answered, "'If (Your) Presence does not go with us, do not lead us up from here.'" Ex. 33:14-15, NAS). But one thing we must realize. There is no such thing as "losing" His presence. Paul tells the Corinthian church twice that "...your body is a temple of the Holy Spirit who is in you" (I Cor.6:19). He also states in v. 17 "...the one who joins himself to the Lord is one spirit with Him." Our body is His temple – His home. He lives in us and our spirit is one with Him! You can't get any closer than that!

So how do we protect our soul from feeling "cold" and away from His presence in our winter season? In the natural, we are told to "layer up", which means wear layers of clothes. The more layers you have on, the more protection you have against the cold getting through. You can actually be warm in the coldest season! So how do we do that spiritually?

In Ephesians chapter 6, the Apostle Paul talks about putting on the "full armor of God" (v.11 & 13). In other words, don't go into battle against the enemy naked! We need to protect ourselves against the "cold" onslaught of the enemy who is always trying to "freeze" us out of our relationship with our Papa God.

Paul first admonishes us to "gird our loins". "Loins", as used here, in the original Greek is defined as "the loin, externally, i.e. the hip; internally by extension, pro-creative power" (Strong's Concordance, Gr. #3751). In other words, our private, most intimate area. That is the first area we are to protect from the cold during our winter season. The private, most intimate area spiritually is our love relationship with the Lord Jesus. In fact, Jesus warned that in the last days before His return, "... because lawlessness is increased, most people's love (for Him) will grow cold" (Mt. 24:12, NAS). So Paul says the first "layer" of clothing to put on in our winter season is "truth" (Eph. 6:14). That's the layer nearest the skin, closest to us. We must protect that which is closest to us first, and that is our love relationship with Jesus.

Growing up in the frigid winters of upstate NY, it was common for us to wear a brand of underwear called "longjohns", "long" because they covered from waist to ankles. They were made from thick wool and **really** kept you warm! While it might be freezing outside, you actually could be sweating! Good protection against the cold. That is the way truth functions in our spiritual walk during our spiritual winter season. The most personal attack the enemy will throw at you is that "God doesn't really love you. If He did, why would He have let that (fill in the blank) happen? He could have prevented it, but He didn't. blah, blah, blah". He's been doing that from the beginning of time. He called into question what God told Adam & Eve in the garden: "Hath God really said...?" (Gen. 3:1, KJV). Well, Jesus identified him in John 8:44: "...the devil...does not stand in the truth, because there is no truth in him. Whenever he speaks a lie, he speaks from his own nature; for he is a liar, and the father of lies (NAS)." There you have it. Whenever those thoughts come into your mind, you can pretty much know from whom they came: the father of lies. So if everything he says to you is a lie, then it must be that the opposite of what he says is the truth!

When Jesus was on trial, Pilate asked Him, "What is truth?" (John 18:38 NAS). Jesus had already answered that question – twice. In John 14:6 (NAS), He said, "I am the way, the truth, and the life; no one comes to the Father, but through Me". He is truth! Whatever He says to you and about you is true. There's your "longjohns" to keep you warm in your winter! When He prayed for His disciples (that includes you and me) in John 17, He prayed, "Sanctify them (you and me) in the truth; (Your) word is truth" (v.17, NAS). So everything that Jesus and the Father says to and about us is truth. Anything that contradicts what They say is a lie, simple as that!

So what do they say to and about us? The answer to that is a book in itself, but here are a couple of examples:

"...I have loved you with an everlasting love; therefore I have drawn you with lovingkindness." (Jer.31:3, NAS).

"But now, thus says the Lord, your Creator,...and He who formed you,...; Do not fear, for I have redeemed you: I have called you by name; you are Mine!...For I am the Lord your God, the Holy One of Israel, your Savior;... Since you are precious in My sight, since you are honored and I love you,... Do not fear, for I am with you..." (Isaiah 43:1,3a,4a,5a, NAS).

Did you hear those statements He said to you? He loves you with an everlasting love. That means He has **always** loved you. There was never a beginning, and it will never end! He has called you by your name! You are precious in His sight and He honors you and is always with you – even in your "winter" season, when you can't feel Him! Wow! You just got the greatest Valentine's Day card you could ever hope for!

If you really want "intimate", read the whole book of Song of Solomon. He is the Bridegroom and you are His bride.

This is the truth you must wear closest to you – your heart.

The next thing to put on in your "winter" is the "breastplate of righteousness" (Eph. 6:14). As I write this paragraph, today is January 21st. I live, as I said, on the Alabama Gulf Coast, the main reason of which was to escape the frigid New York winters. So what do we get today? Rain, freezing rain, sleet, and snow!!! In that mess, I went outside to spread mulch around my plants to protect their roots from freezing because we are also under a "hard freeze warning"! Jesus, what are You doing to me? If this is a joke, it's not funny! Fortunately, I brought my heavy winter coat with me when we moved from NY. It is heavy wool with a hood that ties under my chin. It was worn today! I am in my Winter season! But I digress.

The breastplate is like that heavy winter coat. It is worn on the outside to protect you from the harsh winter blasts of cold wind and to keep you warm. That's what mine did. And that's what the breastplate of righteousness does for us spiritually. It protects us from the cold blasts of the enemy's accusations. The word "righteousness" means "equity of character or act, especially Christian justification" (Strong's Concordance, Gr. #1343). It is derived from a word that means "innocent, absolutely holy". The Bible says the devil is the "accuser of the brethren" (Rev. 12:10). He hurls accusations at us about our past. I have heard it said, "When the devil reminds you of your past, remind him of his future!"

When we repented of our sin and accepted what Jesus did on the cross, our sins were removed "as far as the East is from the West" (Psa. 103:12) and God promises He "will not remember your sins" (Isaiah 43:25b). We have "become the righteousness of God in Him (Jesus)" (II Cor. 5:21). That means that, by definition of the word, we are "innocent, absolutely holy" in God's sight. In fact, we have been adopted "...as sons (and daughters) by which we cry 'Abba! (literally, "Daddy") Father!' The Spirit Himself bears witness with our spirit that we are children of God, and if children, heirs, also, heirs of God and fellow-heirs with Christ..." (Rom.8:15b,16,17a). That's who we are! That's our "winter jacket" to wear when the enemy blows his cold wind accusations at us. We wrap ourselves in the warmth of knowing who Papa God has said we are!

Paul then says we must have our feet "...shod with the preparation of the Gospel of peace" (Eph. 6:15). The snow can get pretty deep in NY and many students (including my 3 children) had to walk to school. Fur-lined boots were a necessity, not a luxury. The extremities (toes and fingers) are the most susceptible to frostbite and the first parts of the body to suffer from it. Therefore, they must be given utmost attention and care.

I believe this can be compared to our walk with the Lord. In the spiritual cold season of our walk, our spiritual feet can be the first to be exposed to the enemy's "frostbite". Using temptation, discouragement, or lack of emotion, he will aim at our feet, trying to make us stumble, or, worse yet, give up on our walk with Jesus.

So how do we "keep our feet warm" in our walk with Christ in the winter season? Paul's answer is remembering the "gospel of peace." Gospel means "good news". Peace includes "prosperity, quietness, rest" (Strong's Concordance, Gr. #1515). The opposite of those would be poverty, turmoil, and struggle. If those are characteristics of our walk with Him, then our feet are freezing.

We need to put our boots on and focus on the good news of Jesus and all He has done for us. Review all of the above we have just shared and personalize it – it's good news for YOU! He is our peace (Eph. 2:14). His peace "passes all (human) understanding (Phil. 4:7). Hey, He left you a pair of His peace boots: "Peace I (Jesus) leave with you; My peace I give to you; not as the world gives, do I give to you. Let not your heart be troubled, nor let it be afraid." (John 14:27, NAS). Just as you get dressed in the morning, start your day with Him. I have a painting hanging on the wall of my bedroom. It is of a beautiful stream that is lined on each side with trees, with snow-covered mountains in the background. In the bottom left foreground of the picture is written "In quietness and trust shall be your strength. Isaiah 30:15". Doesn't that just make you feel warm and fuzzy all over?

Finally, we have to wear a hat in cold weather. We are told that most of our body heat escapes through our head (Boy, do I have a pun for that one!). So Paul says to put on the "helmet of salvation" (Eph. 6:17). Strong's Concordance defines "salvation" as "defender" (Gr. #4992). The enemy floods our mind with threats, lies, and judgments. In court, we need a defender – a defense attorney. David said over and over again that God was his defense. Here are the references in Psalms. Look them up. Say them out loud about and to yourself, inserting your name: Psalm 59:9,16,17; 62:2,6; 89:18; 94:22 (KJV). In the New Testament, John said that if we sin (the accusation from the devil), "…we have an Advocate with the Father, Jesus Christ the righteous" (I John 2:1). The word "advocate" means "one called alongside to help", or, a defense attorney! Jesus is your "winter hat" to protect and defend you from the cold lies of the enemy that try to tell you that you are worthless. How can you (or I) be worthless if Jesus is willing to be our defense attorney?

Yes, there is a winter season for all of us in our walk with the Lord. It may manifest differently in each of our lives, but the cold feels the same. But now we don't have to dread our winter season. Jesus provides all the warmth we need because He is our winter outfit! And boy, does He look good on us! Fashionable and warm! And the best part--- One Size fits all!

3

WILL THIS SEASON EVER CHANGE?

By Joe Pileggi

❝On February 1, self-centered and sour TV meteorologist Phil Connors (Bill Murray), news producer Rita Hanson (Andie McDowell) and cameraman Larry (Chris Elliott) from fictional Pittsburgh television station WP-BH-TV9 travel to Punxsutawney, Pennsylvania, to cover the annual Groundhog Day festivities with Punxsutawney Phil, the Groundhog. Having grown tired of this assignment, Phil begrudgingly gives his Groundhog Day report the next day (February 2) during the festival and parade.

"After the celebration concludes, a blizzard develops that Connors had predicted would miss them, closing the roads and shutting down long-distance phone services, forcing the team to return to Punxsutawney. However, Connors awakens the next morning to find **it is February 2 again**, **and his day unfolds in almost exactly the same way** (emphasis mine). Connors can change his behavior, but other people do and say the same things they did and said the previous day, unless Connors changes something. He is aware of the repetition, but everyone else seems to be living February 2 for the first time. This recursion repeats the following morning and the one after that, and over and over again. For Connors, Groundhog Day begins each morning at 6:00 A.M., when he wakes up in his room in a Victorian Bed and breakfast. His clock radio is always playing the same song, 'I Got You Babe' by Sonny & Cher. His memories of the 'previous' day are intact, but he is trapped in a seemingly endless time loop, repeating the same day in the same small town.

[Finally] "He begins to tire of, and then dread, his existence, starting the day by smashing the alarm clock and professing the [nonsensical silliness] of Groundhog Day as a holiday in his newscast."

The above is part of a synopsis (review) of the movie "Groundhog Day". I use it here so that I can ask you the question: Does this describe your life in your winter season? Every day starts with telling the alarm clock to shut up or pounding it into submission. Then it's dragging yourself out of bed, into the shower, get dressed, put on the coffee (or tea for my wife), breakfast, and "Hi ho; hi ho, it's off to work we go"; then return home, make dinner, watch a movie or spend hours on social media, then to bed. The alarm goes off and it's Groundhog Day all over again! It never seems to end.

For me, moral failure in the early years of ministry ushered me into my "winter season". One year into that season, a prophet of God came to our church and prophesied a powerful word over me that God was going to anoint me with an "Elijah- type ministry". What followed was 20 more years of "winter", as I lived out my "Groundhog Day" existence. I did more than "smash my alarm clock against the wall". I despaired of living. I don't know how many times I asked God the title of this chapter: "Will This Season Ever Change?"

If you are in your "winter" season, you may be asking the same question. The answer is "Yes", but the next question is the kicker: When? That's different for all of us. Some of that answer may depend upon us – how we respond in our winter season and how long it takes for us to yield to what Father is wanting to change in us to ready us for our "Spring" season. But assuredly, Spring **WILL** come!

For "Phil Connors" in the movie, his cycle broke when he changed his attitude and began helping other people (ministry?) rather than loathing his "lot" in life. Maybe that's a key. Getting our mind off of our own station in life and seeing those around us as those who are loved by God and for whom Christ died will change our attitude and help us to sense the "warmth" of Spring. The duration of our "winter" may hinge on that transition. For me, it was 20 some years. What will it be for you?

You may be the one to determine that.

When I was given that "Elijah-type ministry prophecy", I was a mess emotionally and spiritually. God had His work cut out for Him to get me ready for its fulfillment. Had He fulfilled it then, I would have "crashed and burned" and it would have been a disaster!

A Biblical example of someone who endured a "winter" season was my namesake, "Joseph", in Genesis. Let's follow him through his winter season and see if his journey parallels ours in any way.

The account begins in chapter 37 when Joseph was 17 years old. It was at this time that God "pulled back the curtain" of Joseph's future, so to speak, and showed him a glimpse of his destiny. It was through two dreams that showed his brothers and parents bowing down before him. Unfortunately, Joseph's youthful exuberance was not tempered with wisdom and he "blabbed" his dreams excitedly to his family. The end result was that it actually began to set the stage for his being "dumped" into his winter season.

What can we learn from this? Special "Rhema" (personal) words from God, whether in the form of prophetic words or dreams/visions, are not always for everyone to know immediately. They are **personal**, God desiring to reveal to **you** an aspect of His plan for your life. It is **your** dream. Be like Mary – who "treasured these things in her heart" (Luke 2:19). Perhaps Joseph's motives were pure – perhaps he shared out of sheer excitement. God had shown him some things and in his youthful exuberance, he wanted to tell his family. With maturity, zeal is tempered with wisdom. Choose carefully those with whom you share the precious things God shows you, and even then only as He releases you to tell them.

The greatest hurt you may ever suffer will be at the hands of your own "brethren" (Gen. 37:23-24). They may, rather than rejoice with you over the robe of righteousness and garment of praise Father has given you, strip it from you, throw you into the pit of rejection and loneliness, and sell you out (cheaply) to the world in gossip and shame in the world of social media. Rather than receive you in the many-colored robe Father made and gave you, they will reject you and speak out against you, citing your past failures as reasons why God cannot and will not ever use you again.

The many-colored robe to me represents the many gifts and talents God has given us as well as our status in right relationship with Him. When God clothes us in righteousness and gives us "beauty for ashes, the oil of joy for mourning and the garment of praise for the spirit of heaviness" (Isaiah 61:3), others who are not experiencing the same level of intimacy with Him may tend to be jealous and speak ill of us. That may increase as we begin to move in the gifts and callings of God on our life. The tragedy is these people who concentrate on our past failure miss the miracle of God's restorative power, which is also available to them.

Joseph made only one mistake – a lack of wisdom. He paid an extremely high price for it – a 13-year "winter season" that seemingly derailed his dream toward destiny. But was it really "derailed", or was it rather detoured? Or better yet, was it a season of preparation **for** that destiny?

In Winter, plant life seems dead. But is it really? No. The branches are producing new buds, preparing for the next season. The sap in the trees has retreated to the roots where it is receiving nutrients from the unfrozen soil beneath the surface and moisture from the Winter snow and rain. What appears to be death is actually a preparation for the "springing" forth of renewed life in the next season.

Joseph is sold into slavery by his brothers. Joseph was from the lineage of promise – Abraham and Isaac. Yet, through the sins of his brothers, and not his own, he was sold to the lineage of the flesh – Abraham and Ishmael (Ishmaelites – Gen. 39:1). Sometimes, through no fault of your own, it seems as though you've been "sold out" by your very brethren to the slavery of the world where the dreams God originally gave you will now never be fulfilled.

So what do you do while you're in "Egypt" (your winter season), while you're in the place where nothing is happening and you're grinding out a living day by day (your "Ground Hog Day") in a place where you know God's perfect will didn't intend for you to be?

First, maintain your relationship/fellowship with God. Genesis 39:2 says, "And the Lord was with Joseph…". There is nothing here that even implies that Joseph was bitter over his circumstances. He loved God and made a conscious decision that he would remain faithful to Him. He maintained open communication with His God and this personal relationship told him that God had not left him; God knew right where he was.

Secondly, be diligent and faithful where you are. Joseph did with excellence all that was given him to do. Verse 3 says, "The Lord caused all that he did to prosper in his hand". God does not prosper laziness. Joseph honored God in his work; God honored him for his faithfulness: "…so he (Joseph) became a successful (prosperous) man" (v.2).

Paul admonishes us in Colossians 3:23, "Whatsoever your hand finds to do, do it with all of your heart as unto the Lord and not unto men". You may not be doing what God has called you to do yet, but be faithful and diligent in what is before you now. Jesus said, "He that is faithful in little shall be made ruler over much" (Luke 19:17; 16:10; Matt.25:21). God is worthy of your best in whatever you do. He can't (won't) give you a world-wide ministry if you can't (won't) spend time with Him every day in prayer and study of His Word.

Soon after Lori and I moved to Alabama from NY, we joined a church in Mobile. I knew no one in Alabama so there were no opportunities for ministry. I really had thought that this move was the transition from my "winter season" into the renewed life of ministry which would have been my "spring season". But after a year of no ministry opportunities, the only offer I had from the church of which I was now a part was to teach a new believer's Sunday School class and a full-time janitorial position. That job included such "spiritual" tasks as vacuuming all the carpets (it was a huge 2-story church so you can imagine the carpeting!), sweeping and mopping all the tile floors, collecting and taking out the trash, and my favorite job of all: cleaning the countless bathrooms, especially the toilets! It didn't take long for my disappointment to turn to anger and then sizzle into bitterness.

The Joseph in Genesis did all his tasks, no matter how menial with excellence that got him noticed and on two separate occasions promoted. **This** Joseph (me) did just the opposite. Although I also did my job with excellence, it was accompanied by a crappy (excuse the pun) attitude.

One day, I was in the ladies' room (please keep reading!) scrubbing the toilets. My anger reached a boiling point and I sat on the floor next to one of the toilets and had a "conversation" with God. I bet I'm the only preacher in the world who can make **that** claim to fame! As I recall, my conversation went something like this:

"So this is why You brought me down here? This is why You told us to sell our house and move over a thousand miles? This is my breakthrough? This is my return to ministry? Cleaning toilets? I had a better job in NY that paid better and I knew pastors there that would at least have me preach for them once in a while. Who do I have to preach to here – the toilets?"

Thankfully, I didn't live during the Old Testament era. If I had, I probably would have been struck dead and the pastor would have had to tie a rope around my feet and drag me out of the ladies' room in order to bury me! That's what happened to a priest who went into the Presence of God with an unclean heart, and he DID have a rope tied around his foot – just in case!

But since this is the age of grace, Holy Spirit responded to my tirade with just one sentence, which was actually in the form of a question: "Why don't you clean this toilet as if I was the One who was going to sit on it?"

I broke emotionally right then and there and sat there weeping and repenting of my arrogance and bitterness. Something changed in my spirit in that moment and I became more like my counterpart in Genesis. Do everything with excellence, period.

Joseph (the one in Genesis) determined he would not waste his life in bitterness over his circumstances and what others had done to him. Rather, he would honor God each day and use it as an opportunity to serve Him. Do you? Do I? Do we agree with Psalm 118:24, "This is the day the Lord has made. (I will) rejoice and be glad in it"? The result of such an attitude is two-fold: 1.) It is a witness to the unbeliever: "...his (Joseph's) master **saw** that the Lord was with him..." (Gen. 39:3), and 2.)

It brings promotion. Verse 4 says, "So Joseph found favor in his (Potiphar's) sight, and became his personal servant; and he made him overseer over his house; and all that he owned he put in his charge." Promotion comes from faithfulness, diligence, honoring God in **all** circumstances, and having a right attitude in those circumstances.

I served in that "janitorial" capacity from 2001-05. I don't know how long it was after my "ladies' room encounter with God" (that still sounds funny) that my promotion came but after that encounter, I didn't care. But it did come. I pastored a church in a neighboring town and God has used me in ministry, including 8 overseas mission trips, ever since.

Never underestimate the Presence of the Lord in your winter season. "And the Lord was with Joseph...". This does not refer to the omnipresence of God in the universe, but the personal, tangible, intimate, One-on-one Presence of God which is established through personal time with Him:

"In Your **Presence** is fulness of joy..." (Psa. 16:11, NKJV).

"He who **dwells** in the secret place of the Most High shall **abide** under the shadow of the Almighty." (Psa. 91:1, NKJV).

"...O Thou Who **inhabitest** the praises of Israel..." (Psa.22:3b, KJV).

Dwelling, abiding, inhabiting all speak of taking up residence in, living in. When you choose to "dwell" in His "Presence", you will live (abide) under His shadow! You have to be pretty close to something in order to be under its shadow. And don't forget the last one: He "inhabits" – lives in your praise. That, indeed, is the recipe for "an early Spring"!

Joseph knew the same personal Presence of his God as Paul cried out for in Philippians 3:10a: "...that I may **know** Him...". That Presence, that personal, daily communion and fellowship with Father will keep you through any "winter season" you may enter, no matter how long it may last. Remember, Joseph's lasted 13 years. Mine lasted 20 years. Yours? Doesn't matter. In **His Presence** is fulness of joy, not the change of your season.

I would like to close out this chapter with a few encouraging words to you, the reader, especially those of you that have identified this as the season you're in.

Do you feel that God has called you to do something for Him? Having that call burning in your heart, have you found yourself "on the shelf" in a solitary place, in obscurity? That's what we have defined here as your "winter season". Why does God have you there? What is His purpose in allowing you to be in the place of no direction, hearing no words of guidance or comfort or purpose from Him? I asked all these questions multiple times. What the Lord has shown me through my "winter season" I will share with you now.

God's primary purpose in allowing us to walk through the emptiness of our winter season **seemingly** (but not really) alone is to develop Godly character in you to conform you into the image of His Son (Rom. 8:29). Who you are and who you become **in** Him is more important than what you do **for** Him.

Because Joseph co-operated with God, God was able to use the obscure times to build Joseph's character with a Godly strength that would be able to withstand the time of testing (Potiphar's wife) that God, not Joseph, knew would come. You don't know what lies ahead; God does. You don't know when the Garden of Eden or the wilderness temptation will come. Adam and Eve weren't ready. Jesus was. He was "led by the Spirit (not the devil) into the wilderness" (Matt. 4:1, NASB). Allowing God to build Godly character (fruit of the Spirit, Gal. 5:22-23) will prepare you for the day of temptation. Joseph developed an intimate relationship with God during the days when it didn't seem to matter so that he could stand for righteousness in the day that it **did** matter. God works the same way today.

Unlike Joseph, I wasn't ready, and the "Potiphar's wife" came along, I fell. I had Holy Spirit anointing on my preaching and I thought that was all I needed. The anointing won't **keep** you if His character is not **in** you. I learned that the hard way.

If you want to have an "early Spring", then spend some time in (with) the **Son**. Set aside some time every day to worship Him, telling Him how much you love Him.

Read, the Word, especially the Gospels and Paul's letters, along with a good devotional. (I have written a 90-day Devotional called *Fearless* that covers the "Fear Nots" in the Bible, showing why we don't have to fear, no matter what may be going on in the world around us. It is available from most online retailers.) Have conversations with Him, even if you don't sense He is answering you. Find and attend a fellowship that embraces His love and Presence more than anything else.

And, oh, by the way, if you are not convinced that He loves you personally, read Song of Solomon. You are the bride. He is the bridegroom. If you can't get excited about His love for you after reading that, check your pulse!

Spring

4

SPRING : A TEEN'S PERSPECTIVE

By Raygan Boster

WARMTH OF THE SON

Coming out of winter, one of the first things that I notice is it starts to get a little warmer. The sun starts to defrost all of the ice and snow that has built up, which is so refreshing.

This can relate to when we start reconnecting with God and we can see a little growth. We start to see the beauty that comes after the long wait and dreariness of winter. Things around us seem just a little more pleasant and joyful. Dead relationships and situations slowly start to come back to life and the Son starts reaching us more and more. Spring brings hope and relief to the long winter. The question "Will things ever change?" is finally answered. Slowly but surely we get to go outside and not be harassed by the harsh cold.

CULTIVATING AND PLANTING

When spring comes around, this is when we start to plant seeds for harvest. This is a very important time to make sure the soil is healthy enough to nourish the seeds first. If the soil is depleted or has weeds, rocks, or parasites, the seed will not grow.

When getting ready to plant seeds in your spiritual life, you must first get rid of all the bad things crowding your heart. For example, pride, hurt, grudges, bad habits, and sin. Then, plant the right seeds. These seeds are similar to what you used to protect your heart in winter. That would be the armor of God, worship, the Word, Christian fellowship and accountability, and prayer. Then you must continue to cultivate these plants as they grow, continuing to put good, healthy things in, while getting rid of new parasites and weeds that find their way in. Without cultivation, the plant will not reach its full potential and will not be able to produce good fruit in the end.

WATERING

Humans and plants both need water to survive. Both are made up mostly of water, so replenishing the water that is lost every day is vital to survival and growth. Without watering a plant, it will stop growing. No flowers will sprout, no new leaves will grow, and it will not get any taller. Similarly, when we do not water our spirit, it will not grow stronger or taller, leading to vulnerability. After a long period of time with no water, the spirit self will wither away. This is where I like to use the phrase "spiritually dead", although God can raise the dead, including your spiritual self.

In addition, when one "waters" a plant with liquids that are unhealthy for it, like soda for example, the plant will die because it is unable to absorb the nutrients it needs. It is possible to water your spirit with things that are bad for you, and now it is so much easier to do now that social media and the internet are so prevalent in our lives. I am sure that everyone has heard this a million times, but no matter how corny it sounds, we have to be so careful about what we let into our lives. Whatever we let in will either help or hurt our spirit, there is nothing that simply won't affect it at all.

THE BEAUTY OF NEW LIFE

Some of my favorite things to see are flowering plants. They are not in full bloom yet, but just starting to emerge. They are growing every day and slowly reaching their potential. It is such a beautiful sight to see. Spiritually, I feel the same way. Seeing myself or others start to "blossom" after hard work and dark times is so incredible. We all know how much goes into growing and becoming better for Christ, and seeing that all come to fruition is so rewarding in itself. However, people rarely stop to truly appreciate it.

I think we all need to slow down and notice when others around us are starting to show the beauty of new opportunities and new and improved attributes they have attained. But we also need to slow down and appreciate this in ourselves as well. We don't often give ourselves the credit we deserve, and seeing how God is starting to work in and through us should be such a celebration, giving thanks to us, but most importantly to God. After all, without Him, none of it would be possible.

5

SPRINGTIME SHOWERS

By Joe Pileggi

Ah, there are so many parallels between the natural Spring season and our personal spiritual season. Let's see, there's the warmer temperatures and chilly nights. Plants that have looked like they were dead are now suddenly bursting forth with new life – buds, flowers, green grass again! You see, they were not really dead -they were just dormant, resting, storing up energy in preparation for the new growing season.

I need to say this right here. Neither have you been dead during your winter season. God allowed it in your life so you could get much needed rest (dormant) and store up (replenish) spiritual energy for the task (destiny) Father has prepared for you.

Spring is also characterized by refreshing rain showers, essential for this new life to flourish, grow and develop into maturity. And, yes, sometimes those showers can contain violent storms! But more on that later.

How we navigate our "Winter" can often determine whether we experience an "early" or "late" Spring. My Dad so often knew which one we were going to experience when I was growing up on the farm. "Gonna have an early Spring this year", he would sometimes say, while other years it would be, "Gonna be a tough Spring this year." And he was often right! How did he know? He could tell by the type of Winter we had. A harsh Winter would often evolve into an early March thaw which would see the tulips and crocuses push their heads through the soil. When we had a mild Winter and hopes were high that this would lead to an early Spring as well, nature would deceive us with an April frost, freeze, and, yes, even a snowstorm. This was especially concerning on the farm, especially if the crops we had planted started to sprout above the soil. That left them at the mercy of the elements, and a sudden return to winter would devastate the crop.

Can you see a spiritual parallel here? How I navigate the harshness of my winter season will determine when my breakthrough into my spring season will occur. I did not handle my harsh winter season well when, at the age of 33, I was told by my superior that, because of my immoral behavior, I would never minister again. I almost took "the easy way out", feeling there was no more purpose for my life, since I believed "ministry" was my call and destiny. Let me tell you something; your "calling", whatever that may be, is not your purpose for living. Being intimately in love with Jesus is why you and I exist, made in His image, carrying His presence and glory, through which others will be influenced to experience the same lifestyle.

So how do you navigate your winter season to get to your spring season? Well, number one, don't do it the way I did. Don't follow your emotions into depression, suicidal tendencies, hopelessness, bitterness, etc. That will keep you in the frozen tundra of winter indefinitely! If you are going through a "harsh winter season", such as the loss of a marriage, a child, spouse, or close family member, or job/career, and the presence of God seems galaxies away, there are steps you can take to gradually "thaw the ground" you are walking on.

First, worship. Put on a worship cd (that's me, old school) or phone app with ear buds, You Tube, etc. and get alone with God. Worship Him with the music or just sit quietly as it plays. Tell Him you love Him. Do not depend on emotion. You may or may not "feel" like doing it or that it is helping. Satan has access to our emotions (not our spirit), so if we depend on our emotions, he will make sure they stay stirred up – the fender-bender is not covered by your insurance, the fear that that nagging pain may be the "big C", etc. Jesus told the woman at the well, that "...the true worshipers shall worship the Father in spirit and in truth..." (John 4:23, KJV). We worship from our spirit, not our emotion.

Jesus also spoke to this same woman about "living water", whereby drinking it, she would "never thirst again" (John 4:14). A scientific website, Svalbardi.com states "The general consensus is that people can survive for around 3 days without water, with estimates typically ranging from two days to a week. Wilderness guides often refer to the 'rule of 3', which states that a person can live for 3 minutes without air (oxygen), 3 days without water, and 3 weeks without food."

So how long can we go without the "spiritual water" Jesus was referring to? Why would I even want to find out? In my experience, when I skip or otherwise omit time in God's Word even one day, I feel it. I get more agitated with people and events as the day goes on. I feel weaker spiritually and temptations become harder to overcome. If I string several of these days together, the consequences become more dire. I am irritable, prone to outbursts of anger, frustrated, and finding myself yielding to temptations. I am spiritually "dying of thirst". Again, quoting Svalbardi.com: "The world record for the longest survival time without water and food is 18 days, achieved by an 18-year-old man in Austria who was accidentally locked in a government facility in 1979. He was in a near-death state when he was discovered." What's your personal "world record" for being without the living water of God's Word? I'm ashamed to say, mine is in the months, not days. And, spiritually, I was in the same condition as that young man in Austria.

When we had an exceptionally dry Spring on the farm, the results were long-term. The crops suffered stunted growth or died altogether. If they survived at all, they produced little or no fruit (corn, hay, oats, etc.) in the harvest season. The same is true for us spiritually. Just as the Spring showers are refreshing and nutritional to both plants and animals, so is God's Word and Presence in our lives. Our spirit can't live without it.

Those Spring showers cause new life to "spring" forth from plants that have laid dormant throughout the cold, lifeless Winter. So it is in our spiritual lives. As we saturate ourselves in worship and the refreshing "Spring" rains of God's written and personal prophetic words, those words of promise that have laid dormant through our winter season suddenly spring forth in new life. Doors of ministry, career jobs, relationships, that have been closed tight suddenly begin to open. A new awareness of His Presence fills each day. Our fellowship with Him comes alive again as we realize He never left us in our winter season. His Fatherly, watchful eye was constantly upon us every day. We now once again begin to "hear" His voice leading and directing us in our decisions and choices: "This is the way; walk ye in it" (Isaiah 30:21 KJV). It puts a "spring" (Wow! How about all those "spring" words?!) in our step; joy returns to our heart and we begin to once again look forward to each day!

The second thing I learned to do to navigate my winter season, as I shared earlier, is trust. As you can tell, Proverbs 3:5-6 is one of my favorite passages in scripture: "Trust in the Lord with all your heart and do not lean on your own understanding. In all your ways acknowledge Him, and He will make your paths straight" (NAS) (into your spring season!). According to Strong's Concordance, "trust" in the Hebrew means "to be confident, sure" (Heb, #982). To me, it means to take God at His word. He said it; that settles it, no matter what the current circumstances look like.

That's the stance Abraham took. Paul refers to him in Romans 4 as one "...who, contrary to hope, in hope believed...And not being weak in faith, he did not consider his own body, already dead (since he was about a hundred years old), and the deadness of Sarah's womb. **He did not waiver at the promise of God** through unbelief, but was **strengthened in faith**, giving glory to God, and being **fully convinced** (emphasis mine) that what He (God) had promised He was able to perform" (vv. 18a,19-21, NKJV)). Abraham was in the physical "winter" of his life. It was impossible for him and Sarah to conceive a child. Knowing that, Abraham **chose** to believe God's promise that he would be the "father of many nations" (v.17) rather than his physical circumstances. That's called trust! "I don't know how You're going to do it, God, but You said it so that settles it as far as I'm concerned."

Trust allows you to rest in God's promise. That's the third thing I learned in navigating my winter season. Jesus invited us to come to Him when we are burdened down and tired and He will give us rest (Matt. 11:28). Hebrews 3:11-4:11 talks about how important it is for us to "enter into His rest." This rest doesn't mean inactivity; it is the fruit of "trust". It no longer matters how long it takes for His promise to manifest, we know it will. "For you have need of endurance, so that after you have done the will of God, **you may receive the promise**" (Heb. 10:36, NKJV, emphasis mine).

But what about when those refreshing Spring showers turn into violent Spring storms? As I write this (March 30, 2022), we are under a severe storm and tornado alert here in Alabama. Yes, Spring can turn violent, too, and very quickly!

Why, when God begins to bring new life and opportunities into our life, does it turn "stormy" all of a sudden? Shouldn't it be a smooth transition?

Well, no. Look at the opposition Jesus (and later the apostles in the book of Acts) faced. The more life they brought to people's lives, the more opposition they faced, to the point of violence and/or prison.

Ever since the Garden of Eden, mankind has been in an all-out war between good (God) and evil (satan). Satan fights every move of God in an attempt to discourage God's people from accomplishing their assignment. That assignment is: "Your Kingdom come; Your will be done, **on earth as it is in heaven** (Matt. 6:10, NKJV, emphasis mine). Scripture, while referring to satan as the "prince of the power of the air" (Eph. 2:2, KJV), also says that "[T]he kingdoms of this world are become the kingdoms of our Lord, and of his Christ; and he shall reign for ever and ever" (Rev. 11:15, KJV). So the war is on! But the outcome has already been decided.

The changing of your season from your "Winter" into your "Spring" is Father renewing His precious Presence in your life. It also involves opening new doors that He has ordained in order to move you into His plan and destiny. But then, in the midst of the fresh Spring "showers" of His blessing, it suddenly turns into a raging storm of difficulty, opposition, and perhaps even tragedy. The storms that raged through our area last night, while bringing much-needed rain, destroyed property and killed 2 people in Florida.

There are two storms recorded in Matthew that illustrate the truth that satan wants to block the accomplishment of God's plan for your life. The first is recorded in chapter 8, vv. 23-27. This account is also recorded in Luke 8:22-25 and it is only in this account where Luke quotes Jesus saying "Let us go over to the other side of the lake" (v.22, NAS). That was the assignment. Has He given **you** an assignment? Something new? The possibility of a new ministry? New job, relationship? He has invited you to come with Him to the other side – the other side of the "winter" doldrums to the freshness and newness of a "springtime" opportunity. And so, with anticipation and excitement you start out – with Him.

But then, the storm strikes. Unexpectedly, but ferociously. Murphy's Law seems to come into play: "If anything can go wrong, it will go wrong." Luke 8:23, in the NAS says, "But as they were sailing along He (Jesus) fell asleep; and a fierce gale of wind descended upon the lake, and they began to be swamped and to be in danger."

Notice, it was while the disciples were moving in obedience to the Lord's command ("Let us cross over to the other side") that the storm blew up. Many times, when opposition comes against us, we automatically conclude that we have stepped out of God's protection due to disobedience in some area of our life. That can certainly be the case. Just ask Jonah!

So when the storms of opposition come in our spring season, that should be the first thing we check. Ask Holy Spirit, "Is something wrong? Is there something in my life that is in disobedience to your Word?"

He will be faithful to point out if there is something out of line – unforgiveness, pride, anger, critical spirit, wrong motive, etc. Deal with any issue He shows you is there. Remember, He convicts; He doesn't condemn! Make it right and you will be ready to move on into "destiny fulfillment" mode!

But what if, when you go before the Lord, there is nothing amiss in your heart, but still the storm of opposition rages? What do you do? Jesus had the answer (as He always does). He spoke to the storm with authority. He rebuked the wind and the waves (Matt. 8:26). The Lord has been teaching me some steps to take to overcome the "Spring showers" that turn into "severe storms".

First, don't allow fear of the storm to overcome your faith in the promise. He has moved you from your cold "winter" season into the "spring" of His refreshing presence and new open doors. Make sure you have recorded and dated His promise the day He spoke it to you. It was in 1984 that a prophet spoke a powerful prophetic word into my life that God was going to anoint me for an "Elijah-type ministry". But there would be a season of "hiding, as it were" (my winter) but then He would bring me forth with great power and authority (my spring). A lot of time elapsed between the two and I went through much discouragement and doubt that the word was even valid. As I shared earlier, I had just been banned from ministry (1983) for immoral conduct. My marriage hung by a thread and I was told I would never minister again, so it was difficult for me to really believe that God was preparing me for an "Elijah-type ministry".

The storm was raging. I felt like the disciples, who awakened Jesus with the words, "Master, Master, we are perishing" (Lk. 8:24). The KJV states it this way: "Carest Thou not that we perish?" Fear overcame their faith. That's what can happen when the Spring shower turns into a storm.

But wait. It says they had to "awaken" Jesus. Jesus was in the storm with them, in the boat, fast asleep! You see, in Jesus' Kingdom, there was no storm, only peace. That's the second thing He taught me about the storm.

Mark's account of this story says that after they awakened Him, "...(H)e arose, and rebuked the wind and said unto the sea, 'Peace, be still.' And the wind ceased, and there was a great calm" (Mark 4:39, NKJV).

Remember, Jesus is "in the boat" with you. That's His presence, His Spirit. You don't have to "seek" Him. He's in you and with you: "For He Himself said, 'I will never leave you nor forsake you'" (Heb. 13:5b, NKJV). Always seek after peace. Peace is where He is and where He wants you to be, because when you are at peace in the storm, it shows you are confident that "...what He (has) promised He (is) able also to perform" (Rom. 4:21).

So focus your mind on Him (and what He has promised you). Isaiah said that God will keep you in perfect peace when you focus your mind on Him alone because when you do, you are putting your trust in God (26:3). That keeps you above the storm.

That brings me to the other storm, the one where Jesus walked on the water to the disciples in the storm. He then invites Peter to step **out** of the boat and walk to Jesus on the water! You know the story. As long as Peter kept His eyes on Jesus, He walked above the storm on the water. But when his attention was distracted and he turned to look at the waves, he began to sink. The meaning here for us should be obvious.

This is the lesson of walking above the storm. Jesus said, in essence, let the storm rage. Step out of your circumstance that is being tossed around and looks destined to be dashed to pieces on the rocks of disappointment, failure, and tragedy. "Look at Me", He seems to say. "Forget the storm. Get in My presence and love on Me. I'm walking toward you and you're not going to drown in this thing. I've got this – and you! Just worship Me, sit in My presence." As you do, suddenly He's in the "boat" (your circumstance) with you. And Matthew records, "And when they (Peter and Jesus) got into the boat, the wind ceased" (Matt. 14:32, NKJV). Yep. Immediate peace when Jesus steps into the picture.

It was 20 years before that prophetic word began to come to pass in my life – a long time to be in a storm, but it is now being fulfilled in my life! Yes, you may be in your spring season, but the promise of the beautiful warm temperatures of His presence and the fresh spring showers of new open doors may have turned into a violent storm of enemy opposition. Stay strong. Hold on to His promise. The fact that the storm has come is proof alone that the greatness of His promise to you is being fulfilled, because if it weren't, the enemy wouldn't bother to oppose it! You are on the road to your destiny! Speak "Peace, be still" to that storm and look unto Jesus, the Author and Finisher of your faith, (Heb. 12:2a), "... being confident of this very thing, that He who has begun a good work in you **will complete it** (emphasis mine) until the day of Jesus Christ (Phil.1:6, NKJV).

You might as well start celebrating now, because it's already a done deal. He has called you to it; He will make sure you pass from your spring season to your Summer – the season of developing fruitfulness!

6

SPRING: NEW SEEDS, NEW HARVEST

By Joe Pileggi

Spring is so exciting! New life; what looked dead for so long "springs" back to life, creating beauty and a sense of new hope. But not only does what is already in the ground spring back to life, there is the planting of new seeds to bring in a new harvest.

The promises God made to you that seemed to die in your winter season now begin to take on new life. New opportunities, new job, new church, new relationships, etc. that God promised you in past seasons now begin to "spring" forth with a renewed hope of being fulfilled (becoming fruitful in your harvest season). These were seeds of prophetic promise that were sown into your heart by God maybe last year, or longer, that now are showing signs of life. Kim Potter, in her blog, *A New Thing Ministries, May 13th, 2022*, says, "...you are now eating the harvest from the seeds you sowed last season." In order to have a continuous harvest of God's fulfilled promises in your life, you must have a continuous season of sowing (planting). Planting God's Word in your heart daily and through fellowship with Him will position you for a continuous season of harvest. God's seasons do not follow a set time-line like our natural seasons. He can keep you in a season for years, like He did me, or transition you quickly from one season to another. "My times are in your hand..." (Psa. 31:15a, NKJV), David acknowledged. Are yours...and mine? Leave the timing in His hands, in the meantime, "...my harvest will depend ENTIRELY on what I sow...Many do not understand the timing involved in sowing and reaping. We don't often sow today and reap today. Or tomorrow. Perhaps not even next month. Our life must be a life of sowing in each season. If it is, we will reap in each season." (Kim Potter, *A New Thing Ministries, May 13,* 2022).

Did you get that? In God's Kingdom, sowing and reaping can be (and should be) done simultaneously and continuously. Amos 9:13 prophesies God's heart to us:

"Behold, the days are coming, says the Lord, "When the plowman shall overtake the reaper, and the treader of grapes him who sows seed; The mountains shall drip with sweet wine, and all the hills shall flow with it." What an awesome promise! God is saying that in **His** season, the plowman (the one who gets the soil ready for sowing) will overtake the one who is reaping the last harvest. God is ready to plant new "seeds" – new promises, blessings, etc., into your life while you are still reaping the last season's blessings! At the same time, the one who is harvesting today's crop (treader of grapes) will overtake the one who is sowing new seeds! In God's calendar, blessing of harvesting and sowing for next season can and will happen together. That's the end result we all want.

That means we have to be constantly sowing while we are enjoying last season's harvest of blessing. "If you are willing and obedient, you shall eat the good of the land" (Isaiah 1:19, NKJV). If you are willing and obedient to sow in the season you are in, you will reap from that sowing in your next season.

The reason sowing and reaping overtake each other is that we are constantly sowing. We don't reap tomorrow what we sow today. Again, Kim Potter says, "No farmer sows his seed in the morning and digs it up the next day because he doesn't see his harvest. Why? He understands the process and he allows patience to have its perfect work (James 1:4). He knows if he continues to water his seed, he *will* have a harvest. He is aware of the process of seed, time, and harvest (Gen. 8:22). He has sown his seed. Now, he will wait and be patient and continue to water his seed, knowing his harvest is coming. He has no doubt. Neither should we.

"He understands his harvest in life depends entirely on what he sows...therefore he sows. So should we." (*A New*

Thing Ministries, May 13, 2022).

Now, what about those seeds? All this talk about seeds; what am I talking about? Speak English! Ok, let's get practical.

God is the ultimate "Farmer". He has the most precious seed – His Word. Look at Jesus' parable of the sower (Lk. 8:5-15). In verse 11, He says "...The seed is the word of God." God can speak to us in many ways, but in our context here, we have been referring to His promises of blessing, His prophetic words spoken over us and His personal, private words He speaks to us in our personal, quiet time with Him.

I journal a lot. I keep my journal beside me while I read the Word each day and if a verse "jumps out at me", I write it down and the impression or thoughts I get about it. Recently I journaled as I read the 23rd Psalm and ended up with 2 pages of notes! I also write down and date prophetic words spoken over me and then review them from time to time. Some have come to pass (past harvest), some are currently coming to pass (present harvest), and some are yet to produce fruit (coming harvest).

It's so important that we don't allow discouragement to set in as we travel our seasons, especially the spring season where we see things beginning to "sprout" (happen) but not ready for fulfillment, and then in our summer season, when we are in "training", maturing, getting ready for that harvest fulfillment. It still hasn't manifested yet and we can get discouraged or frustrated, asking God, "When?" Jesus, explaining the parable of the sower in Luke 8 says the seed planted in "good" soil "bear(s) fruit with patience" (v.15, NKJV). Ugh, patience! Farmers have to wait for the fruit to be mature – ready – to pick. Remember what James said, "But let patience have its perfect work, that you may be mature and complete, lacking nothing" (1:4, NKJV).

You are reading this book, I believe, by design – Father's design. You have a call of God on your life, plain and simple. God has positioned you on one of the 7 "mountains of influence": family, education, business, arts/entertainment, religion (ministry), government, media. You know you're supposed to be where you are. You have a passion for what He's called you to do. But you're in a season of waiting, and you're frustrated. It's like God is pulling back on the reins and not letting you go to fulfill what He called you to do. I know. I spent years there, waiting for my next "season". But let me assure you, it will come. But in **His** time. He knows when you are ready to be launched into His destiny that He has prepared for you. If you run ahead of Him, you may shipwreck a premature ministry and lose the very influence He intended for you to have on your "mountain".

When I was a boy, maybe 8 or 10, on the farm, I came across a butterfly struggling to get out of its cocoon. It was struggling like it was going to die, so I thought I would help it. I peeled the rest of the cocoon away so it could get out and fly. But instead of flying away, it dropped to the ground and died. You see, it needed the struggle to strengthen its body and wings so that it could fly. The cocoon was its food, not its barrier! It was eating its way out of it and the cocoon was its nourishment. What I thought was hindering it was actually preparing it for fulfilling its "destiny and call". The same is true of the obstacles that are seeming to hold us back from moving into the fulfillment of our harvest season.

Abner Suarez, a current day prophet and dear friend, said the following in his July, 2019 newsletter:

"I believe that for many in the Body of Christ, that which you have been believing God for (sometimes for many years) though the answer has been delayed, will not be denied! God will be faithful to fulfill that which He promised in this season. Those who have been believing God to become debt free will become debt free in this season; unsaved family members and friends and the prodigals are coming home in this season; those believing to get married will meet their spouse. Dreams in the heart are manifesting now and delayed advancement and promotion are coming to the people of God in this season. This is a season in the Body of Christ that though the promise has been delayed, it will not be denied!...[E]very promise that has been delayed in you and your family's life will be fulfilled in this season."

So far, we have talked about the seeds of God's promises, both the ones planted in previous seasons and new ones that He plants in our current "spring" season. But, what about seeds that **we** can plant from which we can anticipate a harvest? What kind of seeds should we be planting in our spring season? Well, what kind of harvest do you need?

Galatians 6:7 says in the NKJV, "...whatever a man (or woman) sows, that he (or she) will also reap." That is an easy concept to grasp. I understood it as a boy, growing up on the farm. When we needed to fill our silo with chopped up corn for winter-time feed for the cows, guess what we planted in the Spring...corn seeds! Wow! What a concept! The kind of seeds we plant will give us the kind of harvest we need and are anticipating to receive. We can expect a multiplication of what we planted. That's important! God is a God of multiplication. When we planted a seed of corn, we didn't get an ear of corn with one corn kernel in it. The ear was filled with row after row of corn kernels – hundreds of kernels! That's the way it is in God's Kingdom – overwhelming generosity!

For example, if I need a financial harvest, I must be willing to plant financial seeds into a good-soil ministry (Luke 6:38; 8:8). Then, I must be willing to "water and weed." What do I mean by that? Here in my hometown, we had a very rainy May, but June has been bone-dry. My vegetable garden thrived in May, but the refreshing showers of May could not sustain my plants in the desert-dry June. I have had to water them every evening or morning. Yesterday, we set a new record high temperature of 101 degrees. My poor plants! Despite my having watered them that morning, they were drooping by evening, crying, "Help!" The spiritual parallel is that in our springtime season, we can plant our seeds and they jump off to a great start with the refreshing "watering" of God's Word and Presence. But then, "June" comes. Hot opposition comes against the financial seeds we have sown – unexpected expenses and emergencies. Instead of seeing the increase toward our financial harvest, we're suddenly depleted financially and wonder what happened.

An example of this just happened to us at our home this week. We had just completed our monthly giving into the ministries we support. **That day**, the "bug" guy came and did the quarterly spraying in our house for pest control. A little while after he left, our dog, Abby, a Sheltie (miniature collie) started acting funny. She became very sluggish, limping, and becoming disoriented. She became worse as time went on, swaying and staggering, hardly able to walk. We called the Vet hospital, since it was now evening and our vet clinic was closed. They said we should immediately call the pest poison control hotline and gave us the number. We did and told them the chemical that was used to spray the house and they said that chemical could cause the side effects that we described and that we should take her in to the vet hospital immediately. There was a $75 charge for that call to the pet poison control center. The vet hospital did blood work and observation and 2 hours later said there were no long-term effects but to monitor her for any further reactions. Charge: $136.

The next morning, I called my vet clinic and they said because there was possible chemical poisoning, they wanted me to bring her in. They kept her all day for ob-servation, more blood work and iv fluids. They also said she would be ok. Charge: $417.50. So, within 24 hours of giving into the ministries we support, we paid out $628.50 in unexpected doggie medical bills!

The thought (temptation) came to me that we should hold back on our giving until we could recoup that mon-ey in our budget. But I realized that would be exactly what the enemy would want me to do. Instead, what I **really** needed to do was to "water" those tender plants that started to sprout from my financial seeds.

How do we "water" them in the face of these unexpect-ed emergencies? With the Word (Eph. 5:26). For me, that means looking up Scriptures that talk about God's promises of financial blessing to those who are obedient to Holy Spirit's prompting in the area of giving. Luke 6:38 (NKJV) is one of my favorites: "Give, and it will be given to you: good measure, pressed down, shaken together, and running over will be put into your bosom. For with the same measure that you use, it will be mea-sured back to you." There are so many others. Second Corinthians 9:6-11 explains God's principle of sowing and reaping and verse 10 sums it up by saying, "Now may He who supplies seed to the sower, and bread for food, supply and **multiply the seed you have sown and increase the fruits of your righteousness"** (emphasis mine). God makes this promise of harvest **when we plant** the financial seed He prompts us to plant, so when we enter the summer season of hot, dry opposition from the enemy, we need to pull these verses out and declare them (out loud) over the planted seeds. This is watering our spiritual garden. The following is an example of how I personalize God's promises of blessing over my finances:

"I honor the Lord with my possessions, and with the first fruits of all my increase; so, my barns will be filled with plenty, and my vats will overflow with new wine. Because I tithe faithfully, God will open for me the windows of heaven and pour out for me such blessing that there will not be room enough to receive it. He will also rebuke the devourer (from my finances) for my sake so that he cannot steal what God has intended for my benefit" (taken from Prov. 3:9,10 and Malachi 3:10).

As far as "weeding" the garden, Jesus describes weeds as "...the cares, riches, and pleasures of life..." (Luke 8:14, NKJV). Weeds must be pulled out by the roots or else, as Jesus warns in that same verse, they will "...choke(d)... and bring no fruit to maturity." What a waste of our giving if we allow the "cares of this world" to choke out the harvest of multiplication God has ready to pour out on us!

If we need a harvest in physical healing, we do the same thing. We find the Scriptures that promise our healing, write them in our journal and speak them aloud over our physical condition and claim those healing promises as ours. My wife and I also find that taking Communion (bread and juice) together re-emphasizes what Jesus did to win our healing and "...by His stripes we are healed"

(Isaiah 53:5). Also, as an act of faith for your healing harvest, find someone who needs healing in their body and declare healing over them. You will be sowing healing by doing that, and guess what your harvest will be!

If you need a harvest of relationships, sow into that need. "A man that hath friends must show himself friendly; and there is a friend that sticketh closer than a brother" (Prov. 18:24, KJV).

There are so many more examples, but I think you get the picture. For every problem, God has the answer! Find it in His Word, plant the seed for the kind of harvest you need, water it by journaling and declaring those verses over your "garden" and keep the weeds out. Your garden will not only survive the hot, dry spells of spring and summer but will actually thrive to produce the abundant harvest you need and that He has prepared for you! Remember Isaac: "Then Isaac sowed in that land, (in the middle of a famine – an extended hot and dry season!) and reaped in the same year a hundredfold; and the Lord blessed him" (Gen. 26:12, NKJV).

Yes, it's Springtime! Spring is the season of anticipation, the excitement of seeing new life spring forth and new seeds being planted with the anticipation that God's planned harvest will produce in its proper season! Plant, sow into good soil, see the promises of God "spring" to life in **your** life. Plant the seeds for the harvest you need, nurture and care for them and experience the harvest Isaac did!

Summer

7

SUMMER: A TEEN'S PERSPECTIVE

By Raygan Boster

MATURITY

When plants grow, we refer to it as "maturing." While they are maturing they get taller, sometimes wider, their leaves get bigger and flowers sprout, and their stems get stronger. When they reach maturity, they are at their peak. However, for our spirit, our "peak" does not come until we reunite with Christ in Heaven. We continue to mature every day until then.

With maturity comes strength and wisdom, although it is not always our own. God provides us with strength and wisdom every day. Personally, I have always been told that I am mature for my age. I believe it is because I had to go through a lot of really hard things as a young kid which made me stronger and more knowledgeable than most people my age. That being said, maturing is never easy. It is a grueling process and often takes hurtful situations to help you get to a more mature state of mind. But that is what is necessary in order to make it through the hard seasons of life.

LONG DAYS OF HEAT

In the summer, the days are longer and definitely hotter. The sun usually doesn't fully set until around 8:00 pm. This also means that it doesn't cool down until around this time as well. The intensity and duration of the heat can really exhaust you, including your spirit.

Intense pressure on our faith, purification, and pressure to do the right thing can leave you feeling drained at the end of the day, like a day with the hot beaming sun. However, it is one of the best ways to induce growth for your spirit. Without these things, no fruit would really be produced because no hardships are causing you to push through.

We cannot always be easy-going and laid back in our spiritual walk. But without this heat and the sun, we would not be able to grow properly. But making sure that you are watering your "plant" adequately will help you endure the heat of the season.

DEVELOPING FRUIT

When summer is in full swing, fruit begins to appear. However, it is not ready to be harvested quite yet. It is still in the process of growing and becoming ripe. If it is harvested too early, it will not taste how it should.

The same goes for our spiritual fruit. The fruits of our labor will start to show for ourselves and others to see, but if it is picked too early, it will not be ready. The key is patience, which is a very rare virtue and not easy to carry out. When something seems almost ready to take, it is so easy to just take it prematurely. But it is so important to stay the course, keep cultivating and watering that plant until the time is right. Jumping into situations or relationships before getting the go-ahead from God could be detrimental to what God had planned. It isn't easy to trust God's timing, but the outcome will be so worth it.

PREPARING FOR HARVEST

The preparation is almost just as important as the actual harvest. If you don't have the right tools and knowledge to harvest the correct way, you could ruin all of the things that you have worked so hard for. Digging into the Word and having wise mentors will help you to gain the knowledge on how to use what God is blessing you with and will help you steer clear of wasting it.

Also, clearing out the space in your life in order to be able to hold all of your harvest is important. If you have nowhere to put the "fruit" you harvest, it will fall victim to the climate and wither away. So clean out all of the unnecessary things in your life in order to have space for what is coming.

8

SUMMER: PREPARING FOR HARVEST

by Joe Pileggi

Ah! Summer in Lower Alabama. Temps in the 90's every day with humidity to match! A local weather forecaster calls it "air that you can wear"! It makes you sweat just to breathe.

In Upstate NY where I grew up on the dairy farm, the climate was much different. If it got above 80, we said it was "hot"! Eighty-five was considered a "heat wave" and if it ever hit 90, we thought we had died and gone to the bad place!

Same season, totally different climates; and, with that, totally different growing seasons. Right now, my tomato plants are drooping in the searing heat of our 90- degree sun. I don't know if they will survive or not. Summer can be a hard season for developing the fruit of the Spring sowing. All the hard work of preparing the ground/soil, planting, fertilizing, watering, weeding – boy, I'm getting tired just typing all that! Then, on top of that, last month, just when my plants were sprouting, we got a hailstorm that flattened just about everything (but they did come back – Resilient!). Storms. So much can go wrong in the summer season to ruin the harvest we have worked so hard to cultivate and bring to maturity.

Now, how does all that relate to our spiritual seasons? Let's break it apart and see what Holy Spirit may want to show us.

Our seasons in God always start with a promise – from Him. I "heard" God call me into ministry at 17, at the start of my high school senior year. I was so excited. I couldn't wait to graduate so I could "be the next Billy Graham" (my words). Obviously, I knew nothing about seasons.

A powerful prophet of God and dear friend of mine, Abner Suarez, wrote in his *"Partner Newsletter, June 2019"*: "One of the things I have learned is that often God will speak to us about things to come far beyond the season and circumstance in which we are currently stationed (John 16:13)". If I had known the cycles of seasons (especially the winter ones!) that I would have to walk through to get to my current season in God, I may not have been so enthusiastic to respond to His call.

The Apostle Paul says in I Thessalonians 5:24, "Faithful is He who calls you, and He also will bring it to pass." Do you remember the powerful prophetic word that was spoken over me by the prophet in 1984 that I referred to earlier? It is being fulfilled in my life today. Yeah, it's been a long season from "winter" of 1984 to the beginning of harvest season.

But before we get fully into harvest season, we move from Spring – the season of new beginnings and new life - to Summer, the season of preparation for harvest.

Like I said, it's Summer here in Alabama, and my garden is growing and developing. My tomato plants have small green tomatoes on them, but they're not ripe yet. My cucumbers have flowers but no cukes yet, etc. This is the developing season, the maturing season, the season of preparation.

So what do we do in this season, when God's promise has burst forth with new life and is growing and developing but it's still not manifesting? It hasn't come to pass yet. Again, my friend Abner states, "God delights in anchoring us in promise while also giving us grace to steward the current day. It is our ability to steward the day in which we live that will determine if we receive the promise that God has released to us for the coming season...As we seek to build our lives on the foundation God intends, it is a vitally important truth to recognize that we must correctly navigate the current season to enter into the promise of the next season." (*June 2019 Partner Newsletter*).

In navigating our "summer season," we will face the "heat of Summer." To me, that means opposition, pressure. By now, the enemy sees that God is not done with you. His call is still on your life; your dream has come alive again! Satan cannot touch you, but he can throw obstacles at you to try to derail what God is doing.

Just today, with our 90-degree heat, we just had a "severe thunderstorm warning"- wind, rain, hail. Heat and storms seem to go hand-in-hand in the Summer. Here in the South, Summer is hurricane season, so severe weather is expected.

In the preparation for God's fulfillment of His promise (your harvest season), can you expect anything less from the enemy? In the heat of your summer season, storms will suddenly blow up, seemingly out of nowhere. You're up for the promotion at work that God showed you is coming, when suddenly it goes to someone else. What is **your** storm? Listen to Paul's laundry list of heat-induced storms that attempted to derail his God-given assignment that he was determined to passionately fulfill:

"Are they (his opponents) servants of Christ?...I more so; in far more labors, in far more imprisonments, beaten times without number, often in danger of death. Five times I received from the Jews thirty-nine lashes. Three times I was beaten with rods, once I was stoned, three times I was shipwrecked, a night and a day I have spent in the deep. I have been on frequent journeys, in dangers from rivers, dangers from robbers, dangers from my countrymen, dangers from the Gentiles, dangers in the city, dangers in the wilderness, dangers on the sea, dangers among false brethren; I have been in labor and hardship, through many sleepless nights, in hunger and thirst, often without food, in cold and exposure. Apart from such external things, there is the daily pressure upon me of concern for all the churches" (2 Cor. 11:23-28 NAS).

How's that for a stormy Summer? That would be enough for most of us to throw in the towel. But not Paul! Listen to his triumphant cry of perseverance:

"Not that I have already obtained it, or have already become perfect, but **I press on** in order that I may lay hold of that for which also I was laid hold of by Christ Jesus. Brethren, I do not regard myself as having laid hold of it yet; but one thing I do: **forgetting what lies behind and reaching forward to what lies ahead, I press on toward the goal for the prize for the upward call of God in Christ Jesus**" (Phil.3:12-14 NAS, emphasis mine). That's called perseverance! He's saying, "Devil, you threw everything you had at me, and I'm still standing and moving toward my season of harvest. I am more than a conqueror in Christ Jesus!" That's a no-quit attitude that we must have if we are to possess the promise God has for us in our harvest season.

As I mentioned in my "spring season" chapter, the disciples also faced some storms in their "summer season" working with Jesus. In one (Matt. 14:22-33), Jesus came to them walking on the water. His message to us there is "I'm always on top of the storm. It doesn't control Me.

It doesn't even faze Me." He then calls Peter to come to Him. In a moment of reckless faith, Peter steps out of the boat and, as long as he kept his eyes focused on Jesus, he, too, stayed above the storm. Another lesson for us, or question: Where is our focus? The storm or the Master of the storm? The answer to that may determine whether or not we move from our "summer season" to our "harvest".

A couple years ago, Bethel Music came out with a song, *Raise a Hallelujah.* One line of it says "*I'm gonna sing in the middle of the storm. Louder and louder, you're gonna hear my praises roar.*"

Jesus expected **them** to calm the storm. You see, in Mark's account of this story (Mark 6:45-52), they had just experienced the miraculous multiplication of the 5 loaves and 2 fish to feed the multitude. Jesus showed them how to call on the supernatural Kingdom to over-rule the natural. First, he told the disciples, "You give them something to eat..." (Mk.6:37), challenging their faith. Then He asked them, "What do you have (v.38)?" The meager result further emphasized the impossibility of fulfilling Jesus' initial command in the natural. Then Jesus invokes Kingdom interference into the natural circumstance: "And He took the 5 loaves and 2 fish, and **looking up toward heaven, He blessed the food and broke the loaves**" (v,41, emphasis mine). Then He gave it to the disciples to fulfill His original command ("You give them something to eat"). While the disciples were distributing the food, it multiplied in **their** hands.

Jesus was teaching them that through their faith in Him, they had the power to overcome all natural limitations.

The very next event in Mark records the disciples encountering the fierce storm mentioned above while trying to cross the Sea of Galilee (vv.47-48). They struggled, "straining at the oars" (v.48, NAS); in other words, they were trying to overcome the storm in their own strength. Jesus expected them to exercise the same authority here in the storm that He had given them over the natural realm in the multiplication of the food – a different situation, but dealing with nature, nonetheless. Instead, when Jesus entered the boat and the wind immediately stopped, it says that "...they were greatly astonished, for they had not gained any insight from the incident of the loaves, but their heart was hardened" (vv.51b,52). In other words, they had learned nothing from the miracle that had just happened **in their hands** (the multiplication of the food)! They didn't realize they had authority to command natural circumstances to line up with God's will. It was Jesus who told them to go to the other side, so it was part of the Divine plan, God's will. The enemy stirred up a storm to attempt to stop it from happening.

What was that plan? Jesus was sending them (and He would join them) to Gennersaret, the place where Jesus had delivered the demoniac (who lived there in a cave) from a "legion" of demons (Mk. 5:1-20). After the demoniac was delivered, he asked Jesus if he could become one of the disciples and go with Him (v.18). Jesus told him no, but rather to go back to his hometown and tell the people what God had done for him, which he did (vv.19-20).

Now, as Jesus returns to this area, Mark's account says that "...immediately the people recognized Him" (v.54). The result was that the people ran and carried all the sick people they could find on pallets (stretchers) and set them in the market place so that as Jesus passed by, as many as touched the edge of His garment were healed (vv.55,56). It involved every village, city, and country-side that He entered – an area-wide revival! This is what satan was trying to stop from happening with the storm. But Jesus had told the disciples (the 12 and the 70) that He had given them "...all authority...over all the power of the enemy..." (Luke 10:19). The disciples were still clueless as to the authority they had been given. Are we?

Perhaps Holy Spirit is showing you that this is where you are; He has brought you into your "summer" season. You have moved through your "winter," where you could not sense His presence and nothing was happening; everything seemed "frozen over" in life. Then you experienced your "spring" season, where new life, new hope, open doors, a renewed flow of His Presence, a refocusing of God's plan, call and purpose for your life came back into view. Now you are in your "summer" season where God's purpose and plan are growing and maturing in your life, but no harvest is ready yet. Suddenly, a storm of circumstances blows up, seemingly derailing all that God is doing.

As I write this (June, 2022), America is reeling in an economic downward spiral. Depending on where in the

U.S. you live, you are paying anywhere between 5 – 9 dollars/gallon for gasoline, a dollar more if you need diesel. The inflation rate is in the teens; the stock market as well as the real estate market are crashing. Violence, mass shootings and sexual perversion of all kinds are at an all-time high. Indeed, if this were a hurricane, it would be a "Category 5"! Fear and anger dominate the emotions of most people.

How do we progress through our "summer" season to our "season of harvest" in such an environment? Like me, you may know the "harvest season" God is moving you toward, but it will take time, labor, and money to get there. How can that happen when we now aren't even sure we can pay our bills or buy groceries?

I believe it is in the midst of this "summer storm" that God would have us learn what the disciples learned in the storm mentioned above. There are lessons here that I believe will carry us through into our harvest season.

There are two principles in this storm that jump out at me as requirements in order for us to overcome our storm and move into our harvest season: faith and action.

Faith has to overcome fear in a storm. When Jesus came walking to the disciples on the water, the disciples were terrified, thinking it was a ghost (Mark 6:49). Jesus had to reassure them that it was He who was approaching and there was no need to fear (v.50). At that, Peter's faith rose to the point of action as he asked Jesus to call him to walk to Him on the water as Matthew tells the account (14:28). Faith and action. Faith involves trust. We must "...(be) fully assured (trust) that what (God) had promised, He (is) able also to perform" (Rom. 4:21 NAS). For example, if we truly believe that God is our "Jehovah-jireh" (our Provider), then we must trust Him to do "...exceeding abundantly beyond all that we (can) ask or think..." (Eph. 3:20) even in the economy we currently find ourselves.

What if you sense the Lord prompting you to give a special offering to a ministry that is dear to your heart in this economy? Initially, you might be gripped by fear (of lack), thinking it's not God. The next thing to do is to address the Lord like Peter did. "Lord, is this You? If it is, confirm that this prompting is You. Tell me to trust You to the point that I am willing to step out of the safety of my 'boat' and walk to You on top of this financial storm and obey You." That's the second principle: action. When Jesus told Peter to "Come," he did. He put action to his faith. James says, "...faith without works is dead..." (James 2:20b).

Lori and I have determined that no matter what the financial "storm" is, or how severe it may become, one thing is non-negotiable: our giving. Ten percent of our income goes to the Lord in tithes, and 10 percent goes to giving into other ministries (sowing). That will never change. We have found God to be more than faithful. Like Isaac (Gen. 26:12), when we sowed, even in the time of financial "famine," we have reaped many- fold.

As I pointed out earlier, Peter's success of staying "on top of the storm" depended on where his focus was. As long as he kept his focus on Jesus, he stayed on top of the storm. When he looked away at the huge waves, he began to sink. So once again, I repeat the question: Where's your focus today? There are so many verses that direct us to where our focus should be. A couple that come to mind are:

Proverbs 3:4-5 – "Trust in the Lord with all your heart, and do not lean on your own understanding. In all your ways acknowledge Him, and He will make your paths straight" (NAS).

Psalm 46:1 – "God is our refuge and strength, a very present help in trouble" (NAS).

Philippians 4:19 – "And my God shall supply all your needs according to His riches in glory by Christ Jesus" (NAS).

And there are so many more. Ask Holy Spirit to bring some to your mind and research them and journal them so you can make them a part of your spiritual "exercise program."

After Jesus rescued Peter and brought him into the boat, the wind immediately stopped (Matt. 14:32). That speaks to me of peace. Here are some Scriptures for that:

"Thou wilt keep him (her) in perfect peace, whose mind is stayed (focused) on Thee: because he (she) trusteth in Thee" (Isaiah 26:3, KJV).

(Jesus talking) "Peace I leave with you; My peace I give to you; not as the world (system) gives, do I give to you. Let not your heart be troubled, nor let it be fearful." (John 14:27 NAS).

"Be anxious for nothing, but in everything by prayer and supplication with thanksgiving let your requests be made known to God. And the peace of God, which surpasses all comprehension, shall guard your hearts and your minds in Christ Jesus" (Phil. 4:6,7 NAS).

You see, God is a good Father. He's got us covered in our storm, whatever that may look like. Have faith in (trust) His promises, step out and do whatever He prompts you to do, and pursue His peace.

The same principles show up in the other storm, where Jesus was asleep in the inner part of the boat. Again, the boat represents our life, being tossed around in the upheaval of the world's storm. But Jesus is in us – the inner part of us – His Spirit dwells in us. He's asleep; that represents His peace. Where Jesus is, there is no storm. He waits for us to stand in the authority He has already given us and speak to the storm ourselves: "Peace, be still" (Mark 4:39 KJV).

This seems like so much work! Wow! The summer heat of opposition, the storms of demonic attack. Is this really necessary to get to my season of harvest? Kim Potter, in her daily devotional blog, *A New Thing Ministries*, *May 30, 2022* edition (a dose of daily encouragement worthy of your time at kim@anewthingministries.com) says, "...you can't have a harvest without the work. ... Harvest is work and if you refuse to do the work, you will have no harvest."

"The lazy man will not plow because of winter. He will beg during harvest and have nothing" (Proverbs 20:4).

Proverbs 10:5 says, "He who gathers in summer is a wise son. He who sleeps in harvest is a son who causes shame."

That verse reads like this in The Passion Translation: "Know the importance of the season you are in and a wise son you will be. But what a waste when an incompetent son sleeps through his day of opportunity." Kim points out that the key phrase there is "**know the season you are in.**"

Do you know the season you are in? Despite the heat (drought, famine) or storms you are walking through, are you aware that you may be in your summer season? Are you preparing for your next season, the harvest season, when you will gather and enjoy the manifestation of God's promises, the fruit of your labor over the previous seasons?

So how do we prepare ourselves to enter into our next season, the season of harvest? Again, Abner Suarez, in his *Partner Newsletter, June 2019 issue,* gives several "truths and reflective questions ...as (we) seek to build (our) life with the appropriate foundation and navigate the seasons of life correctly":

- "If I am in the will of God, the Father, Son, and Holy Spirit are never wasting my time.

- Receiving a promise is what activates that promise on my behalf, whether I see it or not.

- How does my mindset need to change to inherit or live out that promise correctly?

- What negative thoughts and mindsets came to the surface of my heart when the promise was released to me?

- Is any action currently required on my part to begin to walk out this promise?

- Am I managing well what is currently my assignment?"

Abner concludes by saying, "...navigate well the season you currently find yourself in...inherit all promises God released in the correct timing and season."

Kim Potter reminds us that "... Isaac, who sowed in (a springtime season of) famine, reaped (in his harvest season) a hundred-fold return that same year (Gen. 26:12). (Isaac) knew the importance of the season, the spiritual season, he was in.

In the natural, all he could see was famine – but he had a Word from God. God had said, 'Sow and I will bless it.' So, Isaac sowed and saw the harvest he was promised" (*A New Thing Ministries, May 30, 2022*).

The summer season can be, and often is, brutal. It's hot, sometimes stormy, and always hard work. But whatever you do, don't give up! As we move into our next season – harvest season – faithfulness will be rewarded, as Isaac's was. As Isaiah 1:19 says, "If you are willing and obedient, you shall eat the good of the land." Summer was our season of preparation for harvest. Now let's go in and possess it!

9

TESTS AND CHALLENGES

by Josiah Tower

Each season we go through is a new level. Here is something the Lord shared with me about new levels we go through in our lives.

Holy Spirit: A new level comes with new challenges

> And new mistakes

> And new victories

> And new testimonies

This is a process. Don't be afraid of mistakes. Don't be afraid of challenges. You have Me so you shall always be victorious.

Uncertainty breeds faith.

For how can you trust me if you know everything?

All I ask of you is that you believe in Me. Because, if you believe in Me, you'll do and fulfill My purpose. Without belief, you can do nothing.

New levels come with new obstacles and challenges that we should not be afraid of. Yet we should be joyful.

James (NKJV) 1:2-4 – "My brethren, count it all joy when you fall into various trials, knowing that the testing of your faith produces patience. But let patience have its perfect work, that you may be perfect and complete, lacking nothing."

James states that our faith shall be tested, and if we pass that test it produces patience and temperance which is one of the fruit of the Spirit. There can't be a testimony without a test. Everything you do in this life will be tested at some point in your life. The test is not for God, but it's for you and it reveals things about you that may need work. Or, it may reveal how much you've grown and developed.

Either way, it's all a test and it is meant to grow us and to show us how much we need the Lord. We can't truly experience who the Lord truly is just by living an easy comfortable life.

I Corinthians 3:13: "Every man's work shall be made manifest: for the day shall declare it, because it shall be revealed by fire; and the fire shall try every man's work of what sort it is."

As 1 Corinthians states, all of our works are tried and tested. And that test is for the glory of God.

So, my brothers and sisters, never get discouraged when trials arise because all that means is that you have an opportunity to depend on our Lord Jesus Christ, because you are needed. Your light is needed. That light that Christ put inside of you will shine because the Lord assures you, that you are held in His hand and the enemy cannot pluck you out because the calling on your life is too powerful for the enemy to take it from you.

Get over those illusions and anxieties, for your life belongs to the Lord, does it not? The Lord has your life because you gave Him your life when you accepted Christ and received Him in your hearts.

So, if Christ is in you, that means He is for you, so who can come against you?

For Christ has all power because of what He did on the cross for us.

Christ is the Word, and the Word does not return void, but shall accomplish that which the Lord pleases, and it shall prosper in the thing whereto He sent it. (Isaiah 55:11).

This is very good news and this is why we should be joyful when trials come. We shall prosper no matter what because the Word, which is Christ, is in us and all it does is prosper because the Lord cannot be defeated. The Lord, our Savior Jesus Christ, is in us. That makes us undefeatable also, because "in all things we are more than conquerors through Him that loved us" (Romans 8:37).

So brethren, knowing this good news, let us always have a posture of victory and not defeat, no matter what it looks like.

Beloved, don't be as the opossum. For when the opossum is met with danger, it plays dead. When our adversary comes to try us, don't play opossum, for playing opossum is a posture of defeat and a posture of defeat is an abomination in the sight of the Lord.

My Brethren, we are not opossums. We are lions, bold and fierce. We are strong and mighty through the power of our Lord Jesus Christ.

May this bless you, and keep you in good spirits knowing that it is well and that no matter what season you go through, you shall prosper and overcome. That is what the Word of the Lord does. It prospers wherever He sends it. We are sent by God to this dark world to be a light that drives out the darkness through Christ.

Autumn

10

AUTUMN:
A TEEN'S PERSPECTIVE

by Raygan Boster

REAPING THE HARVEST

Finally, it is time to reap all that you have sown. It is long and grueling work, but also very rewarding. Now is not the time to give up. Everything you have waited for is finally available to you; God's timing is here. It is time to use all of the knowledge and tools you have acquired, so don't get ahead of yourself and forget what you have learned thus far. It is common to rush this aspect, trying to do everything at once. You will just tire yourself out. But take it one step at a time; it can't all happen in a day. Also, don't be afraid to ask for help from your leaders and mentors in your life.

As you reap, protect the new fruits in your life. Wash all the dirt and grime off of them and prepare them to be used. This is definitely one of the most encouraging and rewarding times, but stay humble and focused. There is still work to be done.

CHANGING THE ENVIRONMENT

I have always heard the saying that goes something like "you can't rewatch the same movie and expect a different ending". Honestly, as corny as it sounds, it is incredibly true. If you are wanting things in your life to change, you have to change your environment.

Now, a lot of times there isn't much you can do to change your physical environment. Especially when you are younger. You can't always just switch schools or switch jobs. However, you can change who you spend your free time with, change what you watch and what you listen to, and change how you spend your time and money. This is not easy, and takes a lot of determination and discipline. I will say that the effects are so worth it. I have had to change my work environment, my friend groups, and the music I listen to because it was not pushing me towards God at all. It was not easy, but the effect it had on my entire mindset was completely worth it. That is always the number one thing I recommend to anyone when trying to do better spiritually, mentally, or physically.

Change. Your. Environment.

THE BLESSING OF ABUNDANCE

The hard work is done. You have your harvest done and protected. Everything is plentiful and full of life, and you have weeded out the bad fruits from the healthy ones.

Now, look around at all you have in your life and take a second to realize that you could not have done this alone. Don't make the mistake of taking for granted all the blessings you now have because God has blessed you with it. Taking it for granted and not giving thanks to Him could result in a lower harvest next year.

Next, don't let this harvest go bad. Don't let it sit in your storage for too long or it will start to rot and won't be good to use anymore. With the abundance you have been blessed with, don't forget to bless others in need either. Use this blessing for good and spread it to those around you, especially if you know they are in need of it. Blessing others can be one of the biggest blessings to yourself if you do it with the right intentions. Look outwards now, don't keep your focus on yourself in this time of blessing.

PREPARING FOR WINTER

The temperature is slowly starting to drop. What are you to do now?

First, is protection. Protect what you still have of your harvest for use in the winter when the crops and soil are dry. You will definitely need what you have left to make it through winter without struggle.

Next, protect the plants still in the soil. Cover them to resist the cold temperatures and snow. Let the soil recover and become able to provide nutrients for spring.

Next, prepare yourself. Get your "winter clothes" ready and get ready mentally for the challenging season up ahead. You have made it through once; you can and will do it again!

Continue to thank God for the blessings and protection He has bestowed upon you. Remember what He has done for you and know He is still near through the cold. It might seem as if He has abandoned you, but He has not, and the "Son" will shine again.

11

AUTUMN - YOUR HARVEST SEASON

by Joe Pileggi

F inally! We've made it. It's Fall, Autumn, Harvest Season – whatever name we want to give it. We've finally arrived! Not that this is the end of the journey; it never is. God is cyclical. He works in our lives in cycles. When we have come full circle, He's not finished. He always has more for us. But more on that later.

I asked Holy Spirit what would be a good theme verse to start this chapter with. Immediately what came to my mind was Galatians 6:9 (NKJV) – "And let us not grow weary while doing good, for in **due season** (harvest season!) we shall reap if we do not lose heart: (faint not," KJV).

Two words stood out to me in that verse: "weary," and "faint" (KJV). In Strong's Concordance, "weary" is defined as "to be (bad or) weak, i.e. (by implication) to fail (in heart)" (Gr. #1573). It turns out that "faint" is a derivative of "weary" and means "to relax, literally or figuratively; faint" (Gr. #1590). In my paraphrase, I believe Paul is saying that if we don't get discouraged and quit, we **will** reach our harvest season and enjoy a harvest. In other words, don't give up. You may be only 3 feet from your finish line (harvest).

That last statement takes me back to my high school days. I went out for track and ran the 440 (yds.). It was the toughest race because you had to go all out – once around the track, ¼ mile, full speed. We were up against the toughest school in our division and we were beating them. All we had to do was win one more event – the 880 yd. relay (1/2 mile) where each runner goes half way around the track at full speed, then hands off the baton to the next runner. Our anchor (the last runner to takes it to the finish line) wasn't there that day so we had to use Frank, our best runner, to hold the anchor position. I didn't do so well on my leg so by the time Frank got the baton, we were behind. Now, I need to mention the weather conditions. It was terribly cold and a sleety rain was falling. Muscles can tighten up quickly in those conditions.

Frank was awesome. He took the baton and made up ground immediately. Coming around the final turn, he put on a burst of speed and charged into first place. We screamed encouragement to him from the sidelines. All he had to do was cross the finish line and we would win the whole track meet! Frank had a strained, painful look on his face as he gave one final burst of speed to cross the finish line. His muscles were tightening up. Then, 3 feet from the finish line, his muscles seized up and he fell on his face inches from the finish line. We lost. We were stunned. Frank had to be carried off the field into the locker room where heating pads were applied to his legs until his muscles loosened up.

Frank didn't quit. He gave it everything he had and fell (literally) just short. This is what Paul is talking about. The "finish line" is your "due season." That phrase also stood out to me. "Due", in Strong's Concordance (Gr. #2398), is defined as "pertaining to self, i.e. one's own; by implication, private or separate." "Season" is defined as "an occasion, i.e. set or proper time" (Gr. #2450). Paul is saying that God has a personal, private, set, appointed time for your harvest season! Among all the billions of people God deals with, you are that special to Him. You have an appointment with the King! It is a personal, One-on-one private meeting where He answers all the "Whys and Whens" of your seasons. This is your time, your audience, just you and Him.

The summer season can be long, hot, and seemingly unending (especially here in Alabama). In June of this year (2022), we went through a 10-day heat wave with no rain and temperatures near or at 100 degrees every day. Then came the flip side – cooler temperatures but rain every day, which just made the humidity even more stifling. I remember thinking, "Is this season ever going to change? Where's the fresh, cool air of Fall?" It seemed like it would never get here.

It you're stuck in your "summer season" of hot opposition and storms of attack, this chapter is the encouragement you've been hoping and praying for. God has something for you beyond your present season. Kim Potter addresses this in her June 23rd, 2022 blog entitled *"Beyond the Present Season"* (*A New Thing Ministries*):

"...we should never judge ourselves based on a certain season.

"Sometimes we go through seasons where we think we must be doing something wrong. We may ask ourselves, why else would all these hard circumstances come against us? How could all this be happening if we are in the will of God?

"...you can be in the perfect will of God for your life and go through difficult times."

Kim concludes by saying, "I don't know where you find yourself today. Perhaps it is the opposite of what you believe God has promised you. I have been there (so have I!). If that is the place you find yourself, do not judge yourself or your future based on *this* season (Summer?). His promises for your life **will** (emphasis mine) come to pass. Simply hold on to the Word of God and His promise.

"Psalm 66:12 tells us that God may allow us to go through hard seasons, but He will ultimately bring us out into a place of *rich fulfillment* (our harvest season!).

"If where you are today is not what God has promised, it is not your final destination. His promise fulfilled *is* your final destination. The place of rich fulfillment is your final destination. Look past this present season and into the promises of God." [All comments in ( ) are mine].

My question is, how do I transition from my long, hot summer season to my harvest season of God's promises? My answer, and I believe **the** answer is worship! In the midst of the heat of opposition and the storms of enemy attack, I must "seek peace and pursue it" (Psa. 34:14b). I do that through worship, both in music and in words of adoration to the Lord. I put on a worship cd and sing along with the songs if I know the words and just listen in silent worship if I don't. Sooner or later, His "...peace that passes all understanding" (Phil. 4:7) enters my spirit and speaks "Peace, be still" to my storm. He can then speak to me in His "still, small voice" and reassure me that "I've got this!" That voice is speaking to me right now; want to join the conversation?

"Jesus said to them (and us), Come away with Me. Let us go alone to a quiet place and rest for a while..." (Mark 6:31, Worldwide English Translation).

"Come to Me, all (you) who labor and are heavy laden, and I will give you rest" (Matt. 11:28, ESV).

"And He (God) said, 'My presence will go with you, and

I will give you rest'" (Ex.33:14, ESV).

"He makes me lie down in green pastures. He leads me beside still waters. He restores my soul (Psa.23:2-3a, ESV).

"Peace I leave with you; My peace I give to you. Not as the world (our circumstances) gives do I give to you. Let not your hearts be troubled, neither let them be afraid" (John 14:27, ESV).

"For thus said the Lord God, the Holy One of Israel, 'In returning and rest you shall be saved; in quietness and in trust shall be your strength...'" (Isaiah 30:15a, ESV).

Then He gets really personal with me: "I have loved you with an everlasting love; Therefore I have drawn you with lovingkindness" (Jer. 31:3b, NAS).

By now, I have long forgotten the heat and storms of my summer season and I can worship Him in "the beauty of holiness" (Psa. 96:9) and "in spirit and in truth" (John 4:24, KJV). Now I can flow easily into what Paul advises us to do: "Speaking to yourselves in psalms and hymns and spiritual songs, singing and making melody in your heart to the Lord, Giving thanks always for all things unto God and the Father in the Name of our Lord Jesus Christ" (Eph. 5:19-20, KJV).

I now realize that, as Kim Potter says in her May 18th, 2022 blog, I've "Come Full Circle". She explains that "To come full circle means you have completed a cycle or season...This long, hard (Summer?) season is past, and we press on to the new season in God." That's harvest season!

I believe the very fact that you are reading this book is Holy Spirit's way of telling you He is taking you into your harvest season! It's time for you to begin to harvest from all of your hard labor. Jesus said in Matthew 25:23, "His master said to him, 'Well done, good and faithful servant. You have been faithful and trustworthy over a little; I will put you in charge of many things; share in the joy of your master.'" You have been faithful through the hard seasons of your frozen Winter, the hard seed-sowing season of Spring, the hot stormy Summer of opposition and attack. Now, Holy Spirit is saying, "There is an inheritance and it's ready for the picking" (Kim Potter, A New Thing Ministries, June 8th, 2022).

Kim goes on to say, "...we are in that set time...we are in a time of harvest,...the picking or reaping time is here...It is time for believers in God, those who have been found faithful in God, to reap their harvest...This blessing...is the blessing of obedience.

"Isaiah 1:19 says, '*if you are willing and obedient, you will eat the good of the land.*' Increase, our reward for labor has come! It is our time to receive and take possession of our inheritance and all that entails.

"Psalm 16:6 says, *the boundary lines have fallen for me in pleasant places; surely, I have a delightful inheritance.*"

Kim concludes by quoting Bill Johnson: "It's one thing for us to know what belongs to us, it's quite another for us to have possession of it."

How do we "take possession" of the harvest Holy Spirit says is ours? If someone bought a parcel of property and gave it to you, how would you know it was yours? You would have to have a deed stating that the property was bought and paid for and ownership was being transferred to you. When you take possession of the deed, the property officially, legally, and physically becomes yours. You now own that property. Likewise, the promises God has spoken over you, both from His written word and through personal prophetic words, are your "title deed" to your inheritance, your harvest. You gather that harvest in through declaration, the words of your mouth. Jesus said, "...he (you) shall have whatsoever he (you) saith" (Mark 11:23,KJV). Proverbs 18:21 says, "Death and life are in the power of the tongue: and they that love it **shall eat the fruit thereof** " (KJV, emphasis mine).

I journal prophetic words that have been spoken over me as well as Scripture verses that "jump out at me" when I read them. I personalize these words and declare (speak) them out loud using the "I" pronoun to emphasize that Holy Spirit has spoken these words to me, personally. What they promise is **mine**, and that is my "title deed" of possession to that which has been promised – even if I haven't seen it manifest in the physical realm yet. I "harvest" it now because God has said that it is my season for harvest.

Our words cannot be just empty words of hope, like, "OK, I'm going to say that I have this promise and I hope it works," like turning the ignition of your car and "hoping" it will start. Our words have to be an outgrowth of our faith and belief that the promise of God really **is** ours and that it is really our time (season) to harvest it and claim it as our inheritance. They must be words that call forth the manifestation of that which has been planted and nourished in our spirit in the previous seasons and is now ready for harvest. Remember, Jesus said in Mark 11:23 & 24 that if we do "...not doubt in (our) heart, but believe that those things (we) say will be done, (we) will have whatever (we) say. Therefore I (Jesus) say unto you, whatever things you ask when you pray, believe that you receive them, and you will have them."

Paul said of Abraham in Romans 4 that Abraham "... did not consider his own body, already dead (since he was about a hundred years old), and the deadness of Sarah's womb. **He did not waver at the promise of God** (emphasis mine) through unbelief, but was strengthened in faith, giving glory to God, and **being fully convinced that what He (God) had promised, He was also able to perform** (vv.19-21, NKJV, emphasis mine). Are you "fully convinced" that what God has promised you in your spring season He is able to perform it in your harvest season? The KJV uses the phrase "fully persuaded", which, according to Strong's Concordance, (Gr. #4135) means, "*to carry out ful-*

ly (in evidence), i.e. completely assure (or convince), entirely accomplish: - most surely believe, fully know (persuade), make full proof of." No room for doubt in **that** definition! God gave Abraham the promise of a son when Abraham was 75 years old. It was fulfilled when he was 100! There were quite a few "winter, spring, and summer" seasons in those 25 years, but Abraham never doubted God. Sarah did and that resulted in Ishmael. The lesson there: Never settle for an Ishmael ("God will hear") when you've been promised your Isaac ("laughter")!

In the light of declaring our harvest, I want to share with you an entire prophecy given by my friend Abner Suarez in his September, 2019 newsletter. Not only is it appropriate for our current subject, but Lori and I have been declaring it over us since we received it and now are enjoying the "harvest" of it in our personal lives. Through Holy Spirit, Abner said:

"**My beloved, do not grow weary in well doing, for you are entering a season of reaping your due reward. For this is a season of acceleration, expansion, and of producing fruit for the Kingdom of God as never before. This is a season to reap the fruit of your fasting, intercessions, quick obedience and declarations. The enemy has tried to get many to grow weary in this season and caused them to be moved by what they see, but I say to you do not be moved by what you see or what you have even heard in the media** but only be moved by what you hear Me speak in this season. Only be moved by what you hear from Me! Stand on My word and stand in what I have spoken! Declare what I have spoken.

"Some of you stand at a crossroads in this season in your life, but I say to you that I have not left you alone. Lean into Me for wisdom, for this is a season of unprecedented wisdom in the earth for My people; wisdom to navigate the season you now find yourself in, wisdom that if applied, will navigate the next 15 years of your life, wisdom for breakthrough long ago believed for, wisdom to birth nations, changing ministries, wisdom to begin businesses, wisdom to begin businesses in which there are currently no markets.

"This is a season for the Body of Christ to advance the Kingdom of God through the uncommon display of the wisdom of God. The nations of the earth are waiting for the uncommon display of the wisdom of God through the people of God representing His wisdom. So, lean into My wisdom and learn to discern words from My mouth. As you learn what heaven is speaking, declare what heaven is speaking in this season. Declare over yourself, declare in your life, declare over your family, and see quickly the manifestation of what I am speaking in this season. For this is indeed a time of great acceleration for My people, but they must choose to live

above the chatter of the kingdoms of the world if they are to embrace the full purposes of heaven in this season." (Accessed from For Such A Time As This, Inc.; www.abnersuarez.com.).

I believe that word is self-explanatory and needs no commentary from me other than if you sense Holy Spirit saying a "yes" to you as you read it, then embrace it and latch onto every word because it's His "Rhema" (personal) word to you for your current season.

Jesus and Paul both said "...in the mouth of two or three witnesses let every word be established" (Matt.18:16b; II Cor. 13:1b, KJV). In other words, if 2 or 3 (or more) prophetic words are given by people who are unaware of each other, at different times and different places, chances are it can be confirmed that this is God's word for us in this season. I now include several additional words from several other prophets and men of God that strongly parallel Abner's word given in 2019.

The next two appear in Kim Potter's devotional blog, *A New Thing Ministries*, in the entry for March 28th, 2022, entitled "It's Time – It's Our Time". She prefaces them by saying, "There is no better time to believe God than now. Not only believe God, but it's also time to get your hopes up – way up."

John Bevere: "**The promise God gave you is not a tease. You may be finding it hard to have faith when you have faced one disappointment after another.**

"Perhaps you keep replaying the mistakes you've made and now you feel disqualified from His promise. Maybe you've even given up on the promise altogether and it's now just a distant memory. Just checking in to remind you that your hope is in Jesus, not the natural. He is faithful, even when we're faith-less. The natural may make it seem impossible, but God reminds us that 'every word that comes out of [His] mouth does not come back empty-handed' (Isaiah 55:11). There is no better time to believe again than today. Choose faith in the character of God. Stand firm in Who He is: faithful."

Kim's second article was a post from *Elijah List* entitled "Access Granted" where Andrew Towe describes a vision God gave him and the explanation of it. The vision is of someone approaching a large door wanting to enter through it but the first two times he attempts to do so a large red digital sign appears stating "Access Denied". But on the third attempt a large green digital sign appears with the words "Access Granted." Mr. Towe then relates what the Lord told him the vision meant:

"I heard the Lord say, "I am opening doors that have been inaccessible in the past. This is not the time for My Church to stop or be denied. There is an acceleration to prayers being answered. Pick back up the promises you have laid down because of past disappointment. This is a set time for NEW THINGS to come forth. It is a time

for the resurrection of words that you thought had been aborted. They are still alive. Use your mouth and prophesy to the dead things, and I will breathe life into them...The word of the Lord to you today is this: The place where you have been stopped and remained stuck will suddenly shift and change. God is granting you access to walk through doors where you once faced denial and rejection.

"This is your 'set time' for God's favor to manifest in your life."

I am reading a book entitled <u>Understanding Jesus</u>, by Joe Amaral. In it, he describes the words and deeds of Jesus in the light of the first century Jewish culture, which brings so much insight and context to much of what He said and did.

Today I was reading the section on the Feast of Unleavened Bread and how it was to be observed to remember how God delivered Israel from Egypt suddenly, so suddenly, in fact, that they didn't have time to add yeast (leaven) to the baking process of their bread. I will let Mr. Amaral tell the story from there, along with its application for us today:

"The Israelites were in bondage for 430 years. Every day it was the same thing, but on this day something happened that was different, something that was unexpected.

"Perhaps you can identify with Israel at this point in

their journey. Perhaps you have been praying for something for so long that just like the Israelites, you may have stopped believing it was going to happen. Every day they cried out to God for a deliverer to set them free from their oppressors and God, seemingly, did not reply. When they least expected it, when they were at their end and thought it would never happen, God came through for them. I want you to take courage; I want you to be strengthened. Never give up! Never stop believing! You serve a great and mighty God. You serve the God of Abraham, Isaac, and of Jacob. Keep believing and pressing in. Know that your deliverance is sure and that it is near. As you pray and as you seek, He will deliver you. May your deliverance be as quick as it was for the Israelites." (Understanding Jesus, Faith Words, Hachette Book Group, 2011, pp.163-164).

All of these encouraging words speak of a new season that you are entering, a season of abundant harvest. This is the season of God's favor over your life.

Earlier, Andrew Towe made the statement, "This is your 'set time' for God's favor to manifest in your life." Jerry Savelle lists "Ten Benefits of (God's) Favor":

"1. Favor produces supernatural increase and promotion (Genesis 39:21).

2. Favor produces restoration of everything that the enemy has stolen from you (Exodus 3:21).

3. Favor produces honor in the midst of your adversaries (Exodus 11:3).

4. Favor produces increased assets, especially in the area of real estate (Deuteronomy 33:23).

5. Favor produces great victories in the midst of great impossibilities (Joshua 11:20).

6. Favor produces recognition, even when you seem the least likely to receive it (I Samuel 16:22).

7. Favor produces prominence and preferential treatment (Esther 2:17).

8. Favor produces petitions granted even by ungodly civil authorities (Esther 5:8).

9. Favor causes policies, rules, regulations, and laws to be changed and reversed to your advantage (Esther 8:5).

10. Favor produces battles won which you won't even fight because God will fight them for you (Psalm 44:3)."

Strong's Concordance says that "favor" as used here in the O.T., means, "pleasure, desire, delight, favor. The noun... comes from a verb... meaning "to be pleased with" or "to be favorable toward something" (Heb. #7521, 7522).

You see, because you are God's child, He is pleased with you; He takes pleasure in you; He delights in you. If that is hard for you to accept, check out this verse: "The Lord your God in your midst, the Mighty One, will save; He will rejoice over you with gladness, He will quiet you with His love; He will rejoice over you with singing" (Zeph. 3:17). Especially pay attention to that last line – "He will rejoice over you with singing". That word "rejoice" there contains the suggestion of "dancing for joy" or "leaping for joy" since the verb originally meant "to spin around with intense motion" (Strong's Concordance, HEB. #1523). Can you picture Jesus "spinning around with intense motion" and "leaping" and "dancing for joy" when you come into His presence? Well, if not, picture it, because that's what this verse is telling you. That's how overjoyed He is with you! You have won His heart and you have His favor!

You have now entered your season of harvest – abundant harvest. Lay claim to it. Declare it – out loud. This is your "set time," your appointed time to reap what you have sown, into your family, loved ones, finances, everything! Your time has come. Rejoice with the Lord – He is dancing over you with joy. Go ahead, dance with Him. He would love to have you as a dance partner. In fact, He's asking you, "Can I have this dance?"

There is one more harvest I want to mention and that would be the harvest that is closest to the heart of God – the harvest of souls. We are experiencing the greatest ingathering harvest of souls right now that this planet has ever seen. Mario Murillo is conducting tent revival meetings throughout this country and is reporting thousands flooding the altars to give their hearts to Christ. He says he has never seen such a hunger for God in this nation as he is seeing now.

If you have loved ones without Christ that you have been praying for, maybe for years, this is the season for their harvest. Jesus said, "Do you not say, 'There are still four months and then comes the harvest? Behold, I say unto you, lift up your eyes and look at the fields, for they are already white for harvest! And he who reaps receives wages and gathers fruit for eternal life, that both he who sows and he who reaps may rejoice together. For in this the saying is true: 'One sows and another reaps.' I sent you to reap that for which you have not labored; others have labored, and you have entered into their labors" (John 4:35-38, NKJV).

His instructions to us are clear: "Then He said to them, 'The harvest is great, but the laborers are few; therefore pray the Lord of the harvest to send out laborers into His harvest'" (Luke 10:2, NKJV).

So, Jesus has given us a 2-part assignment. First, we are to pray that He send more laborers into this final great harvest. Second, we are to "volunteer" to be one of those laborers that He will send and ask Him what His specific assignment is for us to co-labor with Him in reaping this great harvest, including those loved ones that you have been praying for. Then, love those people into the kingdom. Don't preach at them. They already know they're sinners. The old saying, "They don't care what you know until they know that you care." Bring them into a love encounter with the King of Kings! They want to know that somebody loves them enough to lay down their lives for them. Let them know that Somebody already has!

When you pray for them, make it personal. Pray for them by name and declare them for the Kingdom. Speak it over them (in your prayer):

"Lord, I claim _____ for Your Kingdom today. Give _____ an encounter with Your love. Let me be an instrument of that love through my words and actions that will cause _____ to see You and Your infinite love for _____. Give _____ such a hunger for You that _____ will not be able to resist You. By faith, I harvest _____'s soul for your Kingdom now. Let Your love overwhelm _____ and draw _____ to Yourself. I thank You for it now in Jesus' Name."

Yes, the harvest season has arrived, for you personally and for the multitudes of lost souls who are finding the One who loves them with an everlasting love, gave Himself for them, and will fill the emptiness in their hearts with His love and promise that He will never leave them or forsake them.

So, what season are you in? It really doesn't matter, because each season is coordinated and ordained by Him, led by Him and will ultimately lead to your harvest season! A man much wiser than I wrote a long time ago, "To everything there is a season, A time for every purpose under heaven:" (Eccl. 3:1).

Enjoy the season you are in. You have these promises from the One who brought you there: "...lo, I am with you always, even to the end of the age" (Matt. 28:20b, NKJV). Then Paul reminds us, "For He Himself has said, *'I will never leave you nor forsake you'*" (Heb. 13:5b, NKJV). So go ahead, do a little dance with Him – nobody's watching!

12

IT'S HARVEST TIME!!

by Lori Pileggi

Harvest time is a wonderful thought. You get to enjoy the fruit of your labor. You get to share with others the blessing of harvest. But, harvest doesn't come without a price.

Every calendar year starts off in January - winter. In the northern states of the U.S., the winters can be brutally cold. We spent many years in Western New York, so I know of what I speak.

The air is so cold that it feels as if the hairs in your nose freeze. Your breath hangs in mid-air like tiny crystals shining in the sun. That's cold.

In our lives, we all have times of winter. Times that cause us to feel alone, isolated, forgotten. Times where we feel that God has forgotten all about us and has left us to walk alone.

Times like this can be initiated by many things: financial hardships, anger, and among other things, can be a spouse's confession of unfaithfulness. This happened to us, and it left me falling into a deep depression.

The day after I heard the agonizing information, I lay on the bed. I am usually an optimistic and upbeat person, but now, I could feel myself sinking deep into a dark pit of despair with no return. I didn't have the strength to pull myself out. I was alone. At least, that is what I thought at the moment.

But GOD!

Psalm 107:10, 13, 14 says, "Some sat in darkness and deepest gloom, imprisoned in iron chains of misery...'Lord Help!' they cried in their trouble, and He saved them from their distress. He led them from the darkness and deepest gloom; He snapped their chains." I had no strength to even call upon God. But he listened to my groaning.

It seemed when I was about to go over the cliff of no return, I heard a voice! It wasn't the voice of God. It was the voice of our youngest child calling to me. "Mommy!" "Mommy!" As I listened, I knew I had to pull myself up and go to my child. I got up, wiped my tears and went into our boys' bedroom. Our son was not there. I knew he was at school. God used what He knew would break the grip of the claws of the enemy on my mind and emotions. The voice of my child!!!! Had I not listened to what the Lord sent, I know that our family would have been destroyed!

I went to the Word and read in the Psalms. Psalm 23 "... Though I walk through the valley of the shadow of death I will fear no evil for you are with me..." I felt like we were walking in the shadow of death. Death of our marriage. Destruction of our family. Was it going to die? At that moment all I knew was that God was going to be with us during this dark journey, and we would make it through because God was walking with us.

That winter season was a difficult one. We walked it for quite some time. But winter seasons are like that. They are cold and hard, like the ground under the snow. Nothing grows. Things are frozen. It seems like things will never warm. But spring IS coming.

The earth begins to warm as the sun melts the snow. It sends a message to the frozen ground – it's time to thaw. It's time to become pliable again. It's time for things to grow. Soon, lilies and crocuses peak their heads out of the dirt and show their beautiful faces.

Holy Spirit does that to us in our spiritual life. As we weather the frozen winter of adversity and heartache, Holy Spirit begins to pour His warmth onto our cold hearts and minds, allowing a new perspective to be birthed. Through prayer and forgiveness, cold hearts are warmed and begin to show new life. Fruit of the Spirit begin to become evident: love, joy, peace, patience, kindness, goodness, faithfulness, gentleness and self-control (Galatians 5:22). Spending time in the Word of God renews our minds, and our perspective changes.

Sure, there are other winter seasons that we walked through. But, as we submitted to God, asking Him to change us individually, and praying for each other, God did a mighty work in both of us.

As the sun warms the earth, and seeds are planted, the seeds sprout and grow to maturity, but it is not yet time for harvest. During the summer, we are privileged to see the fruit grow and mature.

My husband plants a garden each year. He checks the garden daily to assure that the garden has what it needs. We are thrilled when we begin to see fresh vegetables begin to grow and mature. This is when we have to watch for critters that will eat the harvest. It could be bugs, or small animals, like rabbits or mice, or if you are privileged enough to live in the country - deer. But whatever it is, we need to protect the fruit. A fence or netting is useful to keep out the critters.

Our spiritual life is no different. When God begins to produce fruit in us, we must protect it. Proverbs 4:23 says, "Guard your heart above all else, for it determines the course of your life." (NLT).

If we allow the hurts and pains of the past to run through our minds, it will ruin the fruit God is growing in us. It will allow the enemy a foothold in our minds and he will weave a web that will be difficult to get out of. We must "Cast down imaginations, and every high thing that exalts itself against the knowledge of God, and bring into captivity every thought to the obedience of Christ" (II Corinthians 10:5). If we do this, we will allow Holy Spirit to continue to grow our fruit to maturity.

So, now, here we are in our harvest season. We have gone on mission trips overseas, seeing God save and heal many! My husband has had the opportunity to teach pastors' conferences in Tanzania, is currently teaching in a Bible training center here in Alabama, and we are part of other ministries in our area. We work together for the Kingdom to reach others and train disciples as we are instructed in Matthew 28:18-20.

This year, 2022, we celebrated our 51st wedding anniversary.

Life IS hard. But God is good! And through all of our seasons He works with us to assure His plan for our lives will be accomplished. I heard a preacher say that God told him that he was not big enough to ruin God's plans for him.

Be encouraged. No matter what season of life you are in, continue to seek God for His peace and direction. Read His Word to fill you and keep you grounded in Him. Ask Holy Spirit to keep you uplifted and direct you in the way He would have you go.

I leave you with John 4:35, "You know the saying, 'Four months between planting and harvest... But I say, wake up and look around. The fields are already ripe for harvest" (NLT).

The harvest is ready. Are you ready for your harvest?

About the authors

RAYGAN BOSTER

Raygan was born and raised in Mobile Alabama. Her passion is worship. She accepted Jesus at a young age. She loves to sing, dance, and enjoys writing.

Raygan loves God and has been a part of youth and adult worship teams in church and school, and continues her worship in College as part of University of Mobile Choir.

She has participated in Assemblies of God youth fine arts competitions in singing, interpretive dance and writing, winning awards at the state level.

Raygan loves to perform. Acting is also a pass-time that she enjoys. She has had roles in "Hamlet" and "A Christmas Carol", among others, while performing in Mobile in Playhouse in the Park productions.

She attended and graduated from Faith Academy School and is currently attending University of Mobile, studying English and Creative Writing. Her goals are to pursue her PhD in English, teach in a university and to continue to write.

JOE PILEGGI

Joe is an ordained minister and has been in ministry for more than 50 years. He was born again and Spirit filled at the age of twelve. After receiving the call of the Lord for full-time ministry, Joe attended Northeast Bible Institute, now called Valley Forge Christian College in Valley Forge, Pennsylvania. Joe is an avid minister and teacher of God's Word. He is passionate about teaching people to walk in the power and anointing of Holy Spirit.

During his fifty years of ministry he has pastored churches across the United States and worked in various positions in others. Each, as he states it, has been an opportunity to witness spiritual growth in the congregations he has shepherded, as well as in himself.

Joe's work for the Lord has also taken him overseas to work with missionaries in Central and South America, helping in their feeding programs, visiting with families in their homes, preaching in churches and teaching pastors' seminars. In one of his trips to Africa, he conducted Pastors' Schools where he taught local pastors how to personally walk in the supernatural power of Holy Spirit and how to teach their congregations to do the same.

Joe is married to Lori, his bride of 51 years. They have three grown children and six grandchildren. Joe is currently a team minister with Gulf Coast Prayer and Healing Center in Loxley, Alabama where he continues to preach and teach the Word of God.

JOSIAH TOWER

Josiah is a native of Mobile, Alabama. He lives and works in the city. Creativity has always been a passion of his life. He has a vision and goal to use his artistic gift to inspire the world about the wonderful God he serves, Jesus Christ. He enjoys drawing, illustrating, logo designing, music and travel.

LORI PILEGGI

Lori accepted Jesus as Savior at the age of 14 and was called into ministry a year later. She attended North-East Bible Institute where she met, and later married her husband Joe.

Lori has worked beside her husband in the ministry opportunities that God has brought them to, including pastoring churches and mission trips to Guatemala and Tanzania.

Lori has a passion for the sick and hurting, and while ministering in Western New York, she had the opportunity to fulfill a childhood dream of becoming a nurse.

She continued her education through her master's degree in nursing management, and currently works part-time at a local agency assisting the elderly and disabled with services that allow them to stay in their homes instead of long-term care placement.

Lori also helps in the ministry office at Gulf Coast Prayer and Healing Center, using her gift of administration.

She enjoys spending time with her husband, 3 children and 6 grandchildren. Sewing, Knitting and crocheting are hobbies that Lori has been able to take up again now that she is semi-retired.

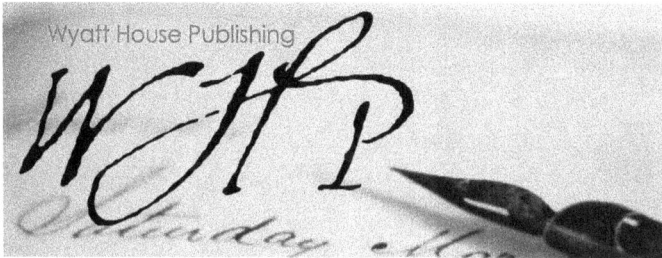

Wyatt House Publishing

You have a story.
We want to publish it.

Everyone has as a story to tell. It might be about something you know how
to do, or what has happened in your life, or it may be a thrilling, or
romantic, or intriguing, or heartwarming, or suspenseful story, starring a
cast of characters that have been swimming around in your imagination.

And at Wyatt House Publishing, we can get your story onto the pages of a
book just like the one you are holding in your hand. With professional
interior design and a custom, professionally designed cover built just for
you from the start, you can finally see your dream of being an author
become reality. Then, you will see your book listed with retailers all over the
world as people are able to buy your book from wherever they are and have
it delivered to their home or their e-reader.

So what are you waiting for? This is your time.

visit us at
www.wyattpublishing.com

for details on how to get started becoming a
published author right away.

www.ingramcontent.com/pod-product-compliance
Lightning Source LLC
Chambersburg PA
CBHW072145090426
42739CB00013B/3284